# 100 GREATEST
# MEN

WITHDRAWN

## Michael Pollard

# Grolier Educational

SHERMAN TURNPIKE, DANBURY, CONNECTICUT 06816

Published 1997
Grolier Educational
Danbury, CT 06816

Published for the school and library market
exclusively by Grolier Educational

© Dragon's World Ltd, 1995

Set ISBN 0–7172–7691–0
Volume ISBN 0–7172–7679–1

**Library of Congress
Cataloguing in Publication Data**

100 Greatest Men
        p.   cm.
    Includes index
    ISBN 0-7172-7679-1 (hard)
    1. Biography. 2. Men--Biography.
I. Grolier Educational Corporation.
CT104.A18   1997
920.71--dc21

                                96-29663
                                    CIP
                                    AC

Editor:              Kyla Barber
Designer:            Mel Raymond
Picture Researcher:  Josine Meijer
Art Director:        John Strange
Editorial Director:  Pippa Rubinstein

Printed in Italy

# Contents

Other great men have influenced the way we think about life and our place in it. Hundreds of millions of people all over the world live by the image of Jesus Christ, Muhammad or other religious leaders. The way in which Greek philosopher Socrates taught his pupils still influences teaching methods today. Another Greek philosopher, Plato, laid down the principle of government that most people believe in today—that the people, not their rulers, should govern.

The message is that greatness can be achieved in many different ways—by action, by invention and discovery, by exploration, by thought, through the arts, or by studying pure science. All the men whose stories are told here earned their place in the history of the world, in whatever field they worked.

One other point should be made. Great women have also played their parts in the achievements of humanity: their stories are told in another book in this series, *100 Greatest Women*.

Michael Pollard

ABOVE: Confucius
BELOW: Martin Luther King

OPPOSITE
TOP LEFT: George Washington
TOP RIGHT: Vincent van Gogh
BELOW: Mahatma Gandhi

# Albert Schweitzer

## 1875–1965

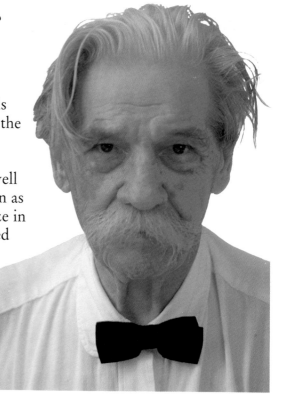

Born in Germany, Albert Schweitzer spent his early life as a musician. However, he gave up the chance of a brilliant career as an organist and music scholar to fight disease in Africa.

Schweitzer was 30 years old, and already well known as a preacher, when he decided to train as a doctor of medicine. He went on to specialize in the study of tropical diseases. In 1913 he sailed with his wife Helene for the part of French equatorial Africa now called Gabon. They built a small hospital deep in the jungle at Lambaréné, with money they had raised themselves. The people of the area had never received proper medical care before. Many suffered from leprosy, a tropical disease that was then incurable.

During World War I Albert and Helene, as Germans in a French colony, were arrested as prisoners of war. Apart from this period, and occasional visits to Europe, the Schweitzers spent the rest of their lives at Lambaréné, caring for the sick and dying. In 1952 Albert was awarded the Nobel Peace Prize for his work. He spent the money on building a village for 300 leprosy victims.

Schweitzer retained his love of music, and particularly of works by the composer Bach. He was given a piano specially built to withstand the climate of the tropical jungle. On his visits to Europe he gave organ recitals to raise funds for his work in Africa.

◄ Schweitzer supervises the building of new huts at Lambaréné. It was hard work, but the locals labored willingly, knowing that Schweitzer gave them their only chance of good medical care.

# Chiune Sugihara

## 1900–1986

During World War II the Nazis rounded up Jews in every country they occupied. Many were killed or taken to concentration camps.

Thousands of Jewish families fled if they could before they were caught. For Jews in Poland, one escape route lay through Lithuania, across the Soviet Union and on to Japan—but they needed Japanese permission to travel there.

In 1940 Japan's chief diplomat in Lithuania was Chiune Sugihara. Japan had not yet entered World War II alongside Germany and Italy, but already had plans to do so. Sugihara's superiors in Tokyo refused to grant permission for the Jews to travel to Japan. They should, he was told, return to Poland.

Sugihara knew that the Jews would face death in the concentration camps if they returned, so he decided to disobey orders. He issued handwritten permits for the Jewish families to travel to Japan. Thanks to his decision, about 6,000 Jews were spared the horrors of the camps. They reached Japan and were then able to travel to the United States.

Sugihara would have liked to have been able to issue more permits, but the Japanese government ordered him to move to a new post in Berlin.

▲ Chiune Sugihara took an enormous risk when he signed thousands of permits for Jews to enter Japan. He was fortunate merely to be moved to another job and not given some more severe punishment.

In 1945, when World War II was over and Chiune Sugihara returned to Japan, he was dismissed from his job for disobeying orders. He lived for the rest of his life in disgrace. Five years after his death in 1986, the Japanese government told his family that it "regretted" its treatment of him.

# Raoul Wallenberg
## 1912–c. 1947

Raoul Wallenberg was a Swede who ran a trading company in Hungary. In 1944 Nazi troops occupied Hungary and began to round up the country's 700,000 Jews and take them to concentration camps. The American and Swedish governments asked Wallenberg to help as many Jews as possible to escape.

Working from Budapest, running huge risks every day, he set up "safe houses" where Jews could stay. They were then issued with Swedish passports. As Sweden was a neutral country in World War II, the Nazis could not prevent holders of Swedish passports from leaving.

Wallenberg managed to escape the Nazis himself, but he was arrested when the Soviet Army occupied Budapest in 1945. He is said to have died in prison.

Did Raoul Wallenberg really die in 1947? No one can be sure. Reports from prisoners who were with him say that he was still alive in the 1950s. Some people believe he may even have been alive in prison as late as the 1970s.

▼ A Jew is forced to walk through the streets with a placard saying, "I am a Jew, but I won't complain about the Nazis."

# Martin Luther King 1929–1968

Until the 1960s, blacks and whites in the southern states of America lived separate lives. They used different churches, schools, parks and even shops. Blacks had to sit separately in cinemas and theaters and on buses.

Martin Luther King was a black clergyman who lived in Montgomery, Alabama. When a black shop worker was arrested for refusing to give up her seat on a bus to a white person, Martin Luther King led a black boycott of Alabama buses. This was the start of his campaign to win equal rights for blacks. Some blacks wanted to attack whites; King argued for a peaceful campaign.

King was arrested and jailed many times, but because of popular pressure in the United States and abroad, gradually, the barriers separating blacks and whites were taken down.

In 1964, Martin Luther King was awarded the Nobel Peace Prize, but he did not live to see his work completed. Four years later, he was gunned down in Memphis, Tennessee, on the balcony of his hotel. Each year, the third Monday in January is celebrated in the United States as Martin Luther King Day.

▶ In 1963 King made his famous "I have a dream" speech, in which he told of his vision of an America where whites and blacks would have equal rights.

# Desmond Tutu
## born 1931

In 1994, when at last South Africa became a nation in which black and white people had equal rights, no one was more pleased than Archbishop Desmond Tutu. He had been praying for this change all his adult life.

Trained first as a teacher and then as a minister of the Anglican Church, in 1984 Desmond Tutu was the first black man to become Bishop of Johannesburg. Two years later he was appointed Archbishop of Cape Town. From his early days as a minister, he spoke out against apartheid—the separation of blacks and whites in South Africa—and pleaded for a peaceful, nonviolent solution. At times, his views were unpopular with both blacks and whites. Many blacks felt that the only answer to white rule was to overthrow it by revolution. Desmond Tutu insisted that the system of apartheid was the enemy, not the white South Africans. But this did not please the white government either, and many times it seemed that Desmond Tutu would be imprisoned.

In 1984 Desmond Tutu was awarded the Nobel Peace Prize. At the award ceremony in Oslo, thousands of students organized a torchlit procession to demonstrate their support for him and their opposition to apartheid.

At last, in the late 1980s, apartheid began to crack. By 1994 it had vanished without a bloody revolution, as Desmond Tutu had prayed it would.

▼ For most blacks, apartheid meant poor living conditions, as in this shantytown near Cape Town.

# The Dalai Lama
## born 1935

In 1937 Tenzin Gyatso, a two-year-old boy from a poor farming family in Tibet, was chosen to become the country's next Dalai Lama—ruler and religious head. Buddhists believe that when people die, they are reincarnated, which means that they return to Earth to live another life. Tibetan Buddhists believe that each Dalai Lama is the reincarnation of his predecessor.

In 1950, the Chinese army invaded Tibet. In 1959 there was a Tibetan revolt against Chinese occupation. The Dalai Lama, along with others who were opposed to Chinese rule, had to flee to India, where he set up a Tibetan government in exile. Since then, the Dalai Lama has worked for the peaceful liberation of his homeland.

▲ Prayer flags flutter near the Dalai Lama's palace at Lhasa. The Chinese have offered to allow the Dalai Lama to return to his home. He has refused to do so unless China gives Tibet back its independence.

In 1989 the Dalai Lama was awarded the Nobel Peace Prize in recognition of his opposition to violence and his determination to restore freedom to Tibet by peaceful means.

# Han Dongfang
## born 1963

In 1989, a television picture shocked the world. It was from Beijing, the capital of China, where tanks were sent to break up a student demonstration against the government. A lone student stepped in front of the tanks to stop them. The picture of this event showed China to the world as a country where the full might of the army was being used against defenseless students.

Not all the people at the protest rally were students. One was Han Dongfang, a railway worker. He had already been in trouble with his trade union for campaigning for Chinese workers to have free trade unions like those in other countries. Threatened with imprisonment, he gave himself up and spent the next two years behind bars.

In 1992, Han Dongfang was released and allowed to go to the United States for medical treatment. When he tried to return to China, the government refused to allow him back. He finally went to live in Hong Kong. From there, he founded China's first free trade union, the Workers' Autonomous Federation.

To the Chinese government, Han Dongfang looks dangerous. But all he wants is for Chinese workers to have trade unions in which they can speak their minds without fear.

> The student protest in Tiananmen Square in Beijing in June 1989 was crushed by fierce attacks on those who took part. An estimated 2,000 protesters were killed as the tanks broke up the demonstration. Afterwards some of the protesters who had been arrested were sentenced to death or to long prison sentences.

▼ From his new home in Hong Kong, Han Dongfang has continued to campaign for free trade unions in China.

# Lao Zi
## c. 600 BC

Lao Zi (old style Lao Tzu) was a scholar who lived in Ancient China. Little is known about his life, but there are many legends about him. One says that he was born by the brilliant light of a falling star. It is also said that, as a baby, he could already speak. He is said to have worked in the Emperor of China's library and to have lived to the age of 110.

The Dao (Tao) religion of Ancient China grew from Lao Zi's ideas. He studied the movements of the Sun, Moon and stars. Because these moved in order, he believed that everything on Earth must also be ordered. Just as people cannot alter the way the Sun moves, so they should not try to alter the regular movement of their own lives. He believed that people should live simply in small farming communities, with each community providing for itself. They should be contented and not always strive for more money or possessions.

▲ The scholar Lao Zi lived some 1,400 years ago, but his ideas are still studied today.

One of the main books of the Dao religion is the *Dao Dejing (Tao-Te-Ching* meaning The Way of Power). No one knows whether it was written, or at least begun, by Lao Zi. Some scholars say it was, but the earliest copies appeared about 200 years after he died.

◀ It is said that Lao Zi went traveling on his own when he was saddened that no one would follow his teachings. But at the Chinese frontier a border guard asked him to write down his teachings. The result, according to this story, was the *Dao Dejing*.

# Confucius
## 551–479 BC

Confucius (known in China as Kong Zi or K'ung Tzu) was a Chinese thinker whose ideas became the basis of China's main religion for over 2,000 years. At the age of 42, he left his job as a government official and became a traveling scholar and teacher. His ideas attracted a group of followers who traveled with him. When he settled in his home state of Lu (present-day Shandong Province) in northern China, his followers formed a community with him as its leader.

Confucius believed that a state like the Chinese Empire was like a family. Just as people in a family should care for each other, so should the Chinese people. The emperor was like the father of a family, and should be obeyed.

The idea that the Chinese should obey their rulers without question was one that appealed to the emperor, who was constantly trying to keep order in his war-torn empire. He therefore encouraged people to listen to Confucius. After the death of Confucius, the philosophy of Confucianism, based on his thoughts, became the main religion of China. It remained so until the last Chinese emperor was overthrown in 1912.

▲ Confucius's idea of the state as a group of people living together peacefully like a family is still influential, even in today's communist China.

◄ Together with a small group of followers, Confucius contemplates the steady flow of one of China's rivers.

It is said that the community led by Confucius numbered about 3,000 students at the time of his death. None of his own writing has survived, but his followers collected many of his thoughts in a book called the *Analects*, or *Sayings of Confucius*.

# Socrates

## 469–399 BC

Socrates was one of the western world's most famous thinkers, but we know about him only through what other people, including his most famous pupil, Plato (see page 18), have written.

Socrates was born in Athens and lived there all his life. He did his teaching in the market place, where he gathered listeners around him. His method of teaching was to question his listeners and then discuss their answers with them. This technique, called the Socratic method, is still used by many teachers in schools and colleges today. One of his main interests was in ideas about right and wrong. Socrates made enemies in Athens, who accused him of making fun of the law and giving young people false ideas. He was tried and condemned to death, but committed suicide.

▲ As this Roman painting shows, Socrates was a fat, ugly man. But he endeared himself to his students, who loved his sense of fun.

▼ Socrates's friends try to persuade him to escape from prison, but he insists that he will take his own life by drinking the deadly poison hemlock.

Socrates was a brave soldier as well as a great thinker. He took part in three military campaigns with the Athenian army, and became famous for his ability to fight on even when his fellow-soldiers were exhausted.

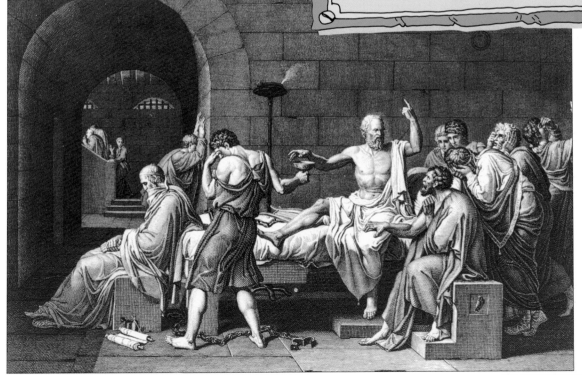

# Plato

## c. 427–347 BC

If the three greatest thinkers of Ancient Greece were to be pictured together, Plato would be in the middle. He was a pupil of Socrates—whose biography he wrote—and the teacher of Aristotle.

Plato was 28 years old when Socrates was sentenced to death. To escape a similar fate, he left Athens with some of Socrates's other followers and spent several years traveling in Greece, Egypt and southern Italy. After ten years he felt it was safe to return, and he founded the Academy in Athens. This was the Western world's first university. Plato presided over the Academy for the rest of his life.

Socrates had been interested in ideas of right and wrong. Plato's main interest was in how ideas of right and wrong could be applied to methods of government. He believed government should be by the people of a state, and not by its ruler alone.

Plato used the Socratic method of posing questions and then discussing them, but he did this in the form of written "dialogues." He wrote more than thirty books. The most famous was called *The Republic*, which is still read by students of politics and philosophy today.

▼ This painting by the Italian artist Raphael shows a sixteenth-century idea of what the Academy was like. Students debate and read; Plato (in red) is at the center.

Plato taught in the Academy for almost fifty years. It continued after his death for another 800 years. By this time, Greece had become part of the Roman Empire. In AD 529 the Academy was closed down by the Emperor Justinian.

# Aristotle

## 384–322 BC

Aristotle was a Greek scholar and lecturer. He took an interest in every branch of learning, from the way people think to the way that objects in the natural world can be classified. Aristotle was one of the founders of Western thought. His works are still studied in Western universities.

Born in Macedonia, the son of a doctor, Aristotle became a pupil of Plato (see opposite) at the Academy in Athens when he was 17 years old. He stayed at the Academy for twenty years until Plato died. Then, feeling he could not work with the new head of the Academy, Aristotle left. After spending five years studying on his own, he became tutor to the 13-year-old prince of Macedonia who was to become Alexander the Great. Finally, in 335 BC, Aristotle returned to Athens and founded his own school, the Lyceum. His lessons were conducted in the gardens of the school, where he walked and talked with his students. He remained at the Lyceum until almost the end of his life.

▼ Aristotle discusses philosophy with his pupil, the young Alexander of Macedonia. Aristotle's published works cover a wide range of subjects—from poetry to natural history.

Some of Aristotle's work has been lost. Most of what has survived is in the form of notes or records of his lectures at the Lyceum. These were published in book form by another scholar, Adronicus of Rhodes, about 200 years after Aristotle's death.

# Niccolò Machiavelli
## 1469–1527

Niccolò Machiavelli was a leading politician and political thinker in the sixteenth-century Italian city-state of Florence. He held some of the highest positions in politics, and this led him to write several books about government, based on his own experience.

The best known of Machiavelli's books is *The Prince*, which was not published until 1532, five years after his death. He intended it as a kind of instruction book for successful rulers. It was probably based on his knowledge of the methods of Cesare Borgia, a ruthless Italian nobleman. Machiavelli looked at different ways of government and at how rulers could seize and hold onto power. He warned against flatterers and traitors. Rulers who want to retain

power must, he said, be prepared to do evil to defend their interests. An effective ruler must be a good warrior, both to fight enemies in his own country and to expand his territory.

Machiavelli turned to writing late in his life. His career as a civil servant came to an end in 1512 when he was dismissed by the Medicis, Florence's ruling family. For a short time, he was put in prison and tortured. In 1513 he retired to a farm to write political books, poetry and plays.

Machiavelli hoped that the ideas he put forward in *The Prince* would encourage a powerful leader to bring the separate states of Italy together to make one nation. This did not happen until almost 350 years after his death.

◀ Machiavelli rests his hand on a copy of one of his books. His writings made the philosopher well known in Italy, and this portrait was painted some years after his death.

# John Locke
## 1632–1704

John Locke was an English thinker whose books had a huge influence on events in Europe and America in the hundred years after his death.

Educated at Oxford University, he spent his working life as an adviser to leading politicians and as a government official. In 1690 he published his two important books. One, *Essay Concerning Human Understanding*, argued that all human knowledge comes from experience. This idea helped develop methods of scientific investigation after Locke's time. The other book, *Two Treatises of Government*, was about how people should be ruled. Locke said that no ruler has the right to go against the wishes of the people, and that a government that deprives the people of their basic rights loses the right to govern. These ideas were startling at a time when the monarchs of the European states believed that they had

been chosen by God and had God's backing for what they did. Both the American War of Independence, which broke out with Britain in 1775, and the French Revolution of 1789 were partly inspired by Locke's ideas.

Locke also wrote about religion, publishing *A Letter Concerning Toleration* in 1689. This work argues that, within reasonable limits, people should be allowed to choose their religion and worship as they please.

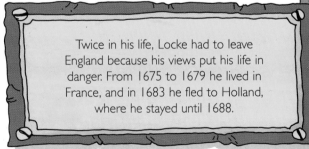

Twice in his life, Locke had to leave England because his views put his life in danger. From 1675 to 1679 he lived in France, and in 1683 he fled to Holland, where he stayed until 1688.

◀ These four engravings show a bust that was carved of Locke towards the end of his life. By this time he had returned to England, where he made friendships with the great scholars and scientists.

# Jean-Jacques Rousseau
## 1712–1778

"Man is born free but is everywhere in chains." These are the opening words of a book published in 1762 which was to change history.

The author was Jean-Jacques Rousseau, a 50-year-old French writer and musical composer. Born in Geneva, he spent his early life doing whatever work he could find. Then he began to make his name as a composer of light operas and as a writer on politics.

His best-known book, published in 1762, was called *The Social Contract*. Rousseau took John Locke's ideas about government (see page 21) and pushed them a stage further. Good government, he wrote, should look after the interests of all the people, the poor as well as the rich. He also wrote a novel, *Emile*, in which he put forward a new theory of education according to which children should be taught by example, in order to bring out their natural abilities.

His ideas were thought to be too radical and revolutionary for the time, so Rousseau fled to Prussia (now part of Germany) after two of his friends warned him that he was about to be arrested.

From then on, his life went downhill. He moved from country to country, at first making friends and then quarreling with them. Finally, when no one would put up with his behavior, he returned to France and scraped a living as a music copyist. Shortly before his death, he became insane.

Ten years after his death, the leaders of the French Revolution were to use Rousseau's ideas and his saying "liberty, equality and fraternity" to overthrow the French monarchy.

Doctors now realize that for the last sixteen years of his life, and perhaps for longer, Rousseau suffered from a mental illness called paranoia. People with paranoia believe that everyone is plotting against them and that people who claim to be their friends are really their enemies.

◀ Rousseau looks at a mountain stream in his native Switzerland. He was one of the first writers to admire the natural beauty of Switzerland's mountainous scenery.

# Karl Marx

## 1818–1883

Karl Marx was a German philosopher who gave the world a new word—"communism." It describes a system of government in which the wealth of a nation is owned by everyone, not just by a few rich people.

After studying law and philosophy, Karl Marx became a journalist in Cologne. In 1843 the newspaper he worked for was closed down because it was too revolutionary. He moved to Paris and then to Brussels, where he began to work with another famous thinker, Friedrich Engels. In 1848 Marx published his *Communist Manifesto*, which called for workers to seize power for themselves.

These ideas terrified the governments of continental Europe, and Marx was ordered to leave Belgium, France and Germany. In 1849 he went to England, where he spent the rest of his life researching and writing. His most

famous book was *Das Kapital*, published in 1867. It forecast that private ownership of businesses by a few very rich "capitalists" would lead to economic chaos, and then the workers would take over. Marx was one of the leaders of the First International, which planned the revolution he dreamed of. However, the First International split up, and Marx's health failed. He died in 1883 without having seen any progress towards the revolution he predicted.

It was thirty-four years after Karl Marx's death that the first Marxist revolution took place. In 1917 communists took over the government of Russia, overthrowing the Tsar. After World War II many eastern European countries and China also came under communist rule. However, during the late 1980s Russia and eastern Europe turned against communism.

◀ The red flags of the communist revolutionaries fluttered outside the Winter Palace in St Petersburg, one of the first buildings to be taken over in 1917.

# Hammurabi

## c. 1792–1750 BC

Babylon was a city of the ancient world, set beside the River Euphrates in present-day Iraq. In 1792 BC Hammurabi became its ruler. During his reign he made the city the hub of an empire that stretched for hundreds of miles through the fertile crescent-shaped territory between the rivers Euphrates and Tigris.

Unlike many rulers of the time, Hammurabi believed in governing his people fairly. He wanted to rule by laws that would apply to all his people— wherever they lived in his empire. He divided the empire into smaller areas, run by local officials. A stele—a pillar of stone—was set up in each area. A list of laws was carved on each stele. These laws, which were to be obeyed by rich and poor alike, became known as Hammurabi's Code.

In 1902 a stele containing the almost complete text of Hammurabi's Code was found by archaeologists at Susa in present-day Iran. It is over eight feet high. The stele also gives an account of the key events of Hammurabi's reign.

Hammurabi's Code contained 282 laws. They dealt with most matters of everyday life, including crime and punishment, trade, marriage, divorce and family affairs, money-lending and payment for goods and services. The legend went that Hammurabi was given the Code by Shamash, the ancient Babylonian sun god, in the same way as, in the Bible story, Moses received the Ten Commandments from the Jewish God Jehovah.

◀ In this bronze statue, Hammurabi kneels before one of the Babylonian gods. The king's hand is in front of his face in an ancient gesture of greeting.

# Alexander the Great

## 356–323 BC

Alexander the Great was one of the most successful military leaders in history. In only twelve years he conquered an empire that stretched across Asia Minor from Greece eastward to northern India and southward to Egypt.

Alexander came to the throne when he was only 20 years old. His father, Philip of Macedonia, had already conquered much of Greece, but some of the Greek states rebelled against Alexander. In a ruthless campaign, he brought them back under his control. Then, in 334 BC, he set out eastward at the head of a Greek army of over 30,000 men.

Alexander swept on through present-day Turkey, defeating the forces of King Darius of Persia. He continued down the eastern Mediterranean coast to Egypt. His conquering army then marched eastward to Persia, where in 331 BC Alexander proclaimed himself king.

In 328 BC he led his men eastward across the deserts and mountains of present-day Iran and Afghanistan to the Khyber Pass, the western gateway to India. He was hoping to reach the end of the world, which he believed lay somewhere beyond. But his troops refused to go any further. Alexander was forced to turn back. He died in Babylon of a fever while planning another campaign.

> Alexander was fascinated by Persia. As the king, he wore Persian clothes, and both his wives were Persian princesses. His first wife, Roxane, had a son, but they were both murdered in 310 BC in the struggle for power that followed Alexander's death.

▼ This illustration from a fifteenth-century book shows Alexander fighting a battle at Ephesus, in what is now Turkey. The artist has given Alexander and his men fifteenth-century costumes and armor.

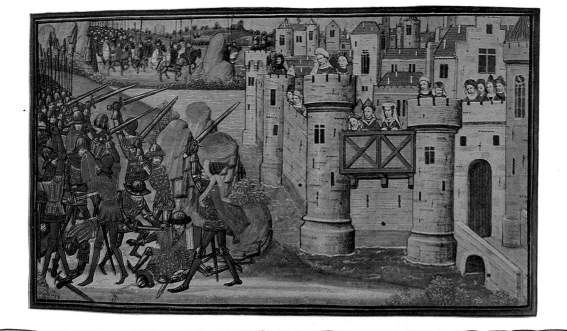

# Asoka
## c. 300–232 BC

In 272 BC Asoka became king of Maurya, an empire covering most of India. Twelve years later he led an attack on Kalinga, an independent state bordering the Bay of Bengal. With the fighting over, and Kalinga conquered, over 100,000 people had been killed.

Asoka felt guilty at such heavy losses and was determined never to be responsible for such violence again. He changed his own life completely. He adopted the Buddhist belief in nonviolence and called himself "the Prince of Peace."

This was not an empty claim. Asoka's empire after 260 BC was governed with care and love. Asoka set up schemes to look after the sick and elderly, and built wayside resting places for travelers on the roads of his empire. At his own expense, he arranged for wells to be dug to bring water supplies to villages that had previously had to bring in their water over long distances. All over his empire, inscriptions on rocks and pillars and in caves told of his conversion to Buddhism, and urged his people to copy him.

▲ This sixth-century sculpture portrays a bodhisattva, one who has reached the high state of enlightenment and who teaches his or her followers.

To celebrate his conversion to Buddhism, Asoka built the Great Stupa at Sanchi in central India. It is a huge stone temple beneath which the ashes of Buddha, who had died 200 years before, were buried.

◄ The fame of the emperor Asoka spread beyond India after his death. He had brought Buddhism to thousands of people and had built shrines and temples all over the subcontinent. One place where he was well known was Tibet, where this painted banner with a portrait of Asoka was made.

# Shi Huangdi

## 259–210 BC

Shi Huangdi called himself "the first Emperor of China." There had been many great rulers before him, but he liked to think of himself as the first emperor of a united China. To support his claim, in 213 BC he destroyed all the records of Chinese history before his reign.

Shi Huangdi became king of the state of Qin in 246 BC, when he was only 13 years old. China was then a group of warring states. His aim was to make it one great nation. He began by ordering that only one language should be written or spoken instead of the many that had previously been used. He ordered that the whole country should obey the same set of rules, even down to the width of carts and the system of weights and measures. Disobedience was punished by death.

Then Shi Huangdi tried to cut China off from the outside world. To the north lay Mongolia, the home of tribes which often made raids on northern China's villages. To keep them out, Shi Huangdi ordered that the Great Wall of China be built. It was one of the most ambitious building projects ever undertaken.

▲ The Great Wall of China was 1,500 miles long and it took twenty years to complete. Over 300,000 slaves worked on it. Since Shi Huangdi's time, the wall has been repaired and rebuilt many times, but it still follows the same course.

Soldiers guarded Shi Huangdi throughout his life —and even after his death. He ordered over 7,500 life-size clay models of soldiers to be placed in his tomb to watch over his body. This "terracotta army" remained there undisturbed until the tomb was discovered in 1974.

◄ When Shi Huangdi died, he was given the most elaborate tomb imaginable. Buried in it was a whole army of life-size figures made of terracotta. All the figures are different—each modeled on one of the emperor's real soldiers.

# Julius Caesar

## c. 100–44 BC

In 60 BC, Rome was introduced to a new kind of government. Three Roman leaders—Julius Caesar, Pompey and Crassus—formed a ruling "triumvirate." Caesar was a member of one of Rome's leading families and already governor of Spain. He was given charge of the province of Gaul, which consisted of southern France. This was the signal for the start of his most famous military campaign.

The Romans in Gaul were constantly under attack from the tribes to the north, and Caesar decided to conquer them. By 56 BC his army had reached the northern coast of France, and in the next two years he twice invaded Britain. He conquered southeastern Britain, but before he could advance further, he had to return to Gaul to put down a rebellion among the Gallic tribes.

Meanwhile, the rest of the Roman Empire was doing badly. Crassus was killed in battle in Asia, and Pompey and Caesar became rivals for the title of Emperor of Rome. Their armies fought, and Pompey was defeated. By 45 BC, Caesar was undisputed Emperor, and announced plans to expand his empire.

He did not have time to fulfill his ambitions. Resenting his power, rivals plotted to kill him, and he was stabbed to death on March 15, 44 BC.

When Pompey was defeated by Caesar, he fled to Egypt, where Caesar followed him and had him killed. During his stay there, Caesar fell in love with Cleopatra, the Egyptian queen, and fought and defeated her enemies. Cleopatra returned to Rome with Caesar, but left after he was murdered. She claimed that Caesar was the father of her son Caesarion.

◀ Caesar's fame was long-lasting. He wrote two books, *On the Gallic War* and *On the Civil War*, which described his campaigns. His triumphs inspired generals and artists for many years, as this eighteenth-century painting shows.

# Charlemagne

## AD 742–814

In AD 771, Charlemagne—also known as Carolus Magnus, or Charles the Great—became king of the Franks. These peoples occupied most of what is now France, Belgium, the Netherlands and part of Germany. He set out at once to expand his empire. By AD 800 his territories extended to northern Spain, the rest of Germany, Austria and parts of Italy.

Charlemagne was a Christian, and forced the people he conquered to become Christians. In gratitude Pope Leo III gave him the title of Holy Roman Emperor, and he was crowned on Christmas Day AD 800. The Holy Roman Empire founded by Charlemagne was to remain a major force in Europe for hundreds of years.

Charlemagne left behind another important legacy. His method of governing his empire was to divide it among his nobles and the bishops of the church. They were given not only the land but also the right to control the lives of the people who lived on it. In return, the landowners promised loyalty to Charlemagne. This system, which is called feudalism, governed the pattern of life in many parts of Europe until the eighteenth century, and in some places later.

▲ Under the feudal system, a knight would support his king or emperor in battle in return for a grant of land. In this medieval manuscript, two emperors (recognizable by their gold crowns) and their armies confront each other on the battlefield.

French, German and Italian literature is rich in legends based on the life of Charlemagne. In many of the stories he appears as a godlike figure with supernatural powers, whose armies were unbeatable.

▶ Charlemagne's conquests brought him honors all over Europe. Here he is being crowned king of Italy, after his conquest of the northern part of the country in 774.

# Kublai Khan
## 1214–1294

Kublai Khan was the grandson of the great Mongol leader Genghis Khan, who led the Mongol conquest of southern Russia, parts of the Middle East and northern China. Genghis Khan was famous for his cruelty, but his grandson was quite different.

Kublai Khan continued the conquest of China started by his grandfather and in 1259 became the first foreigner to become Emperor of China. In 1279 he conquered the Sung Empire and tried to extend Mongol rule into southeast Asia.

Always eager to learn, he adopted the Chinese way of life and set up a magnificent court in the city of Cambaluc, the present-day Beijing.

Marco Polo, the Venetian traveler, visited Kublai Khan there and remained in the Khan's service for seventeen years. He brought back to Europe tales of the splendid banquets that took place in the Khan's palace.

Kublai Khan's greatness lay in turning the ruthless, destructive force of the Mongols like his grandfather to more peaceful uses. He opened up trading links between China and the rest of the world. He encouraged the establishment of the Buddhist religion in China and supported the spread of education. He brought law and order to China, and set up a network of hospitals for the sick.

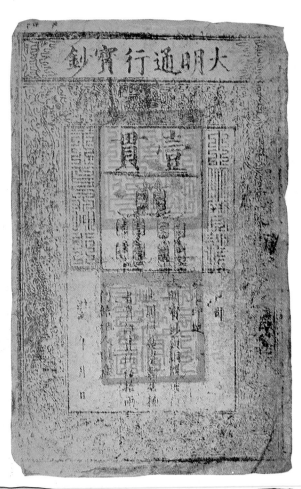

Marco Polo's accounts show how much more advanced life was in Kublai Khan's China than in Europe. There was an efficient postal service, and the Chinese already used paper money instead of gold and silver.

◀ Paper money like this was being used in China and Mongolia long before it was introduced to Europe and the Mediterranean.

# Peter the Great
## 1672–1725

Tsar Peter I of Russia, who became known as Peter the Great, was one of the most feared and admired rulers of his time. He was feared because of his ruthless treatment of anyone who threatened his power. However, Peter the Great was also admired as the man who modernized Russia and made it a great European power.

Before Peter's time, Russia was almost completely cut off from the rest of the world. To the east lay the vast and sparsely populated lands of central Asia. To the south was the Ottoman Empire, which controlled the sea route from the Black Sea to the Mediterranean. Russia's sea route to the west via the Baltic was blocked by the Swedish Empire. In a series of wars, Peter opened up the Black Sea and then the Baltic to Russian ships. He created a navy to protect Russian trading ships.

To mark Russia's new westward-looking ideas, in 1703 Peter founded a new capital city and major seaport at St Petersburg, to replace Russia's old capital Moscow. St Petersburg, at the eastern end of the Baltic, was built on land Peter had won from Sweden.

▲ The main square in St Petersburg, Peter the Great's capital city. Peter ordered many palaces to be built here in the modern, European style.

In 1697, Peter the Great set out on a tour of Europe. Society seemed to him to be much better organized in the West than in Russia. He studied the industrial methods used in other countries, and brought craftsmen back with him to introduce their ways of working into Russia.

▶ Peter the Great was well known for his ruthlessness. He even had his own son, Alexey, shown here with his father, tortured to death for plotting against him.

# George Washington
## 1732–1799

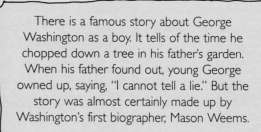

On the last day of April 1789 George Washington was sworn in as the first President of the United States of America. The American states had won their independence from Britain eight years before. Washington as Commander-in-Chief had led the American forces to a brilliant victory over the British and had become a national hero. He had hoped, after the war was over, to return to his family's country estate, but he was persuaded that it was his duty to serve his country again as its leader.

Washington's task was to set up a stable government for the new country. He did this so successfully in his two four-year terms as President that he was invited to stand for a third term. But by this time he was 65 years old. Most of his adult life had been spent in the service of his country and he was tired. He refused the offer of nomination and, in 1797, retired to spend the last two years of his life on his estate. George Washington is still known as "the Father of his Country."

There is a famous story about George Washington as a boy. It tells of the time he chopped down a tree in his father's garden. When his father found out, young George owned up, saying, "I cannot tell a lie." But the story was almost certainly made up by Washington's first biographer, Mason Weems.

▼ Washington has pride of place among the American presidents carved on the rock face at Mount Rushmore, South Dakota.

# Napoleon Bonaparte
## 1769–1821

Born on the Mediterranean island of Corsica, Napoleon Bonaparte was a junior officer in the French army who rose to rule an empire that covered almost the whole of continental Europe. During the 1790s he led the French in many successful campaigns against the Austrians in Italy. By 1799, he was ruling France and, in 1804, he had himself crowned Emperor.

By 1812 he controlled almost all of Europe, either by direct rule or by making alliances with other nations. Then, in 1812, he attacked Russia.

After some early successes, his troops reached Moscow, but were driven back by the fierce Russian winter, with terrible losses. Two years later, Russian, Austrian and Prussian troops entered Paris. Napoleon was forced into exile on the island of Elba in the Mediterranean.

Although Napoleon lost his empire, many of the changes he brought about in France live on. The legal system he set up, known as the Napoleonic Code, is still the basis of French law. Another of his reforms, the metric system of weights and measures, is now used in most parts of the world.

▼ In 1815 Napoleon returned from exile and fought the British and Prussian forces at Waterloo. It was his final defeat.

# Simón Bolívar
## 1783–1830

Simón Bolívar, known as "the Liberator," was one of South America's most famous freedom-fighters. At that time, South America was part of the Spanish and Portuguese empires. Bolívar became a national hero because of the important part he played in gaining independence for the northern states of South America.

Simón Bolívar was born in Venezuela into a noble Spanish family. As a young man he traveled to Europe, and came back fired with the idea of creating an independent United States of South America, similar to the newly independent United States in the north.

He joined the forces fighting for freedom from Spanish rule. In 1824,

after many setbacks, he and his revolutionary army finally succeeded in defeating the Spanish. By then he had become President of Venezuela, Bolivia, Colombia, Ecuador and Peru. It looked as if his dream would be fulfilled.

Bolívar's life ended in disappointment. Many South Americans began to believe that his rule was no better than that of the Spaniards. Some South American states began to quarrel among themselves, and there was civil war in others. The leader who had once been a hero was now hated by his people. In 1830, a sick man, he resigned as President and died the same year.

In 1819, Simón Bolívar led a famous march of 2,500 soldiers across the Andes Mountains to liberate the Spanish colony of New Granada (now Colombia). After braving ice, floods and torrential rain, his army took on a Spanish force twice its size, and won.

◀ Bolívar helped win independence for Venezuela, Colombia, Ecuador, Peru and Bolivia. He did not achieve a United States of South America, but he is still a hero for many people of the region.

# Abraham Lincoln

## 1809–1865

On April 14, 1865, President Abraham Lincoln of the United States went with his wife to the theater in Washington, DC. It was a celebration. The four-year-long Civil War had ended at last, with victory for the northern states over the Confederate south. Halfway through the play, a shot rang out and President Lincoln slumped in his seat. He died the next day. His assassin, John Wilkes Booth, was an actor who resented the northern victory and the liberation of North America's slaves.

Abraham Lincoln was born in Kentucky, the son of a poor farmer. In 1861 he became the sixteenth President of the United States—but the states were no longer united. The south depended for its prosperity on slave labor. When the northern states opposed the extension of slavery into the new states of the West, the southern states broke away to form their own union.

Lincoln decided that the original Union must be saved at all costs, even if it meant civil war. This broke out in 1861. By the time it ended, it had cost the lives of half a million Americans—but the Union was saved, and the slaves were freed.

The New Orleans slave market, one of the busiest in the South, often sent traders to other cities for new stock.

Abraham Lincoln's opposition to slavery dated from a visit he made to New Orleans, in the heart of the slave state of Louisiana, when he was about 18 years old. There, he saw slaves in chains, and the horror of the memory never left him.

▶ John Wilkes Booth kills Abraham Lincoln at Ford's Theater, Washington, DC. Booth's crime was pointless —Lincoln had already achieved his twin goals of freeing the slaves and reuniting the states.

# Mahatma Gandhi
## 1869–1948

Violent revolution is one way of trying to bring about changes in society. Another way is to press for change by nonviolent means. Gandhi, who campaigned for independence in India, believed in the second way.

Born at Poorbandar, Mahatma (Mohandas Karamchand) Gandhi trained as a lawyer in Britain and worked for a time in South Africa. In 1914 he returned to India, which at that time was part of the British Empire. He began working for Indian independence. Some Indians hoped to win independence by force, but Gandhi believed in peaceful means of protest such as fasting and nonviolent marches. This did not prevent the British from imprisoning him many times as a threat to Indian security.

At last, in 1946, the British government agreed to talks on independence, and a year later it was granted. The Indian subcontinent was divided into two nations—the mainly Hindu India and the mainly Muslim Pakistan.

The granting of independence did not stop the violence, however. Hindus and Muslims fought over the way the country had been divided. Gandhi tried to check the attacks in which many were killed by threatening to starve himself to death unless they stopped. In 1948 he became a victim of violence himself when he was murdered by a Hindu gunman.

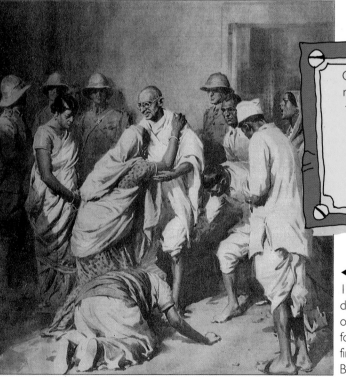

Gandhi, who was given the name Mahatma, meaning "great soul," never used his power to benefit himself. To the end of his life he lived simply, eating plain food and wearing plain, home-made clothes. When independence came, Gandhi did not join the government, but supported his friend Nehru as India's first prime minister.

◄ Gandhi was arrested by the British in 1932 because of his campaign of civil disobedience. But repeated spells in prison only resulted in more widespread support for the Indian leader. His country was finally granted independence from the British in 1947.

# Kemal Atatürk
## 1881–1938

Kemal Atatürk is often called "the Father of modern Turkey." He was born Mustapha Kemal, and adopted his more familiar name only after he had become the first President of the modern Turkish state in 1923.

Turkey had fought alongside Germany in World War I and had been defeated. When the war ended, Greece invaded Turkey and was driven back by an army led by Kemal Atatürk. In 1923 Turkey became a republic, and Atatürk —by now a national hero—was appointed its first President.

He believed that Turkey must turn its back on its Islamic past and become a modern European state. He encouraged western-style dress and forbade men to wear the turban or the fez. He allowed women to appear in public unveiled, and they were given the vote and legal equality. He introduced education for all children and banned the use of the

▲ Atatürk turned his back on traditional garments such as the fez, encouraging his people to leave behind the customs of the past.

> If he had been happy at school, Kemal Atatürk might never have joined the army and would not have become his country's ruler. When he was at secondary school, he disliked one teacher so much that, defying his family, he ran away and secretly signed on at an army cadet school.

Arabic alphabet in favor of the Roman one used in the rest of Europe.

With these changes, Atatürk was trying within a few years to overcome centuries of tradition, and many Turks opposed him. To push through his reforms, he was forced to become a dictator. He remained in total control of Turkey until his death in 1938.

◄ Atatürk became a dictator in the 1930s, in order to push his policies through. But today Atatürk is held in reverence in Turkey, because people realize that his reforms laid the foundations for the modern Turkish state. This is his memorial at Sarikarus.

# Franklin D. Roosevelt
## 1882–1945

Franklin Delano Roosevelt fought a crippling disease to become the thirty-second President of the United States. He was 39 years old when he was struck down by polio. His legs were paralyzed, and many of his friends thought that this was the end of his political career.

But Roosevelt was not so easily discouraged, and in 1933 he became President. In the early 1930s the United States was in the grip of economic depression. Many businesses had failed and millions of people were out of work. Roosevelt aimed to give Americans hope and confidence in the future.

He began a program called the "New Deal." This provided work on projects such as housing, roads, bridges, harbors and hydroelectric schemes. Farmers were helped by cuts in taxes, and business loans were made easier.

The United States slowly recovered, and Roosevelt led the United States into World War II, but he did not live to see victory. He died in April 1945, three weeks before Germany's surrender.

Polio is a serious infectious disease that affected many children before the 1950s, when a vaccine was developed. Those who caught the disease were often, like Roosevelt, permanently disabled. Polio is now rare in developed countries.

◀ Roosevelt, British leader Winston Churchill, and Russian leader Josef Stalin attended the Yalta Conference in the Crimea in February 1945. They discussed the ending of the war and planned how the postwar world would be organized. Two months later, Roosevelt was dead.

# Nelson Mandela
## born 1918

Nelson Mandela was twenty-six when, in 1944, he joined the African National Congress, one of the organizations campaigning for what then seemed the hopeless cause of equal rights for blacks in South Africa. The ANC hoped to make progress by peaceful protest, but its actions met with violent opposition from the police.

In 1961 Mandela, by then leader of the ANC, was arrested with seven other activists and put on trial. Despite a four-hour speech in his own defence, he was sentenced to life imprisonment. For twenty-six years he was imprisoned on Robben Island, off Cape Town.

The world was not allowed to forget Nelson Mandela, however. His supporters constantly reminded world leaders of his plight, and an international

▲ Nelson Mandela spent twenty-six years in prison for his beliefs. During that time, people all over the world campaigned for his release.

The turning-point in South Africa's modern history came on March 21, 1960, in the town of Sharpeville near Johannesburg. Police opened fire on a crowd of peaceful demonstrators, sixty-nine of whom were killed. Soon afterwards, the ANC was banned —but the police attack revealed to the world the brutality of white South African rule.

campaign was organized for his release. By 1990, the political tide was beginning to turn in South Africa. In February of that year Mandela was freed and allowed to resume his political work on behalf of blacks. In 1994 his life ambition was achieved when South Africa became a country in which blacks and whites had equal political freedom—and it was Nelson Mandela who became the first President under the new regime.

◀ Nelson Mandela addresses an ANC rally in South Africa. His lifelong struggle has helped to abolish apartheid and gain votes for black people.

# Mikhail Gorbachev
## born 1931

In 1985, Gorbachev became the political leader of the Soviet Union and saw that great political changes inside and outside Russia were vital. Since the end of World War II, the communist East had been fighting a "Cold War" with the democratic West. Inside the Soviet Union, the economy was inefficient and corrupt. In a series of meetings with President Reagan of the United States, Gorbachev aimed to end the Cold War. Within the Soviet Union, he sought to make industry more efficient—a policy known as *perestroika*.

Gorbachev's policy of open talks, known as *glasnost*, prompted many states in the Soviet Union to demand independence. Eventually, Gorbachev was forced to resign in December 1991.

▲ Gorbachev planned the withdrawal of Russian troops from the countries of eastern Europe. This led to the end of division between East and West Germany in 1989.

Mikhail Gorbachev was quite unlike previous Soviet leaders. He was willing to admit to the failings of communism and was seen in the West as a leader who worked in a similar way to those in the noncommunist world. When traveling abroad, he was willing to give interviews to journalists and was accompanied by his fashionably dressed wife, Raisa.

◀ Gorbachev was forced out of power. But he will be remembered as the man who turned Russia into a more open society and helped remove the threat of nuclear war between Russia and the West.

# Zoroaster

## c. 628–c. 551 BC

Zoroaster founded the religion that was followed by the Persians for over 1,000 years until the Muslim invasion from the west in AD 643.

Little is known about Zoroaster's life apart from a number of legends in ancient Persian writings, known as the *Avesta*. According to these, his religious ideas came to him when he went to live as a hermit on a mountain. The mountain caught fire, but Zoroaster escaped and began to preach the new religion. One of the people he converted was King Vishtaspa of Bactria, the land to the east of Persia (now Afghanistan). He joined Vishtaspa's court, and the king became Zoroaster's protector.

Zoroastrians believe that the history of the world is a long struggle between the spirit of good, known as Ahura

▲ To the followers of Zoroaster, fire and the writings of *Avesta* are of great spiritual importance.

When the forces of Islam invaded Persia, some followers of Zoroaster escaped and fled to the area around Bombay in western India. About 120,000 of their descendants, known as Parsees, still live and practice their religion there.

Mazda, and that of evil, Ahriman. Humans play a part in this struggle by their good or evil actions. When people die, according to Zoroaster, they have to meet an accountant who makes out a "bill" of their lives. The good deeds are in one column and the bad deeds in another. What happens next depends on which list is longer. People with more good deeds than bad go to paradise. The rest go to hell.

◀ This painting shows the figure of Zoroaster engulfed in flames. A new religion was revealed to him when the mountain he lived on caught fire.

# Muhammad

## c. AD 570–632

Muhammad, the founder of the Islamic faith, was born at Mecca in what is now Saudi Arabia, not far from the shores of the Red Sea. He was a merchant, and his travels across the desert brought him into contact with other merchants who talked about religion, and Muhammad began to take an interest in religious thought.

When he was 40 years old and living in Mecca, he began to have visions. Angels appeared before him and told him that God—Allah—had chosen him to preach the true faith. One of Allah's laws was that the rich should give to the poor. This angered the rich, and Muhammad and his followers had to flee to Medina, about 250 miles from Mecca. From there, Muhammad launched a war against the enemies of Islam. By 629 he had conquered Mecca.

His followers carefully wrote down his words when he preached to them, believing them to be the true words of Allah. After Muhammad's death these writings were collected together in the Quran, Islam's holy book.

▲ Mecca, the city where Muhammad was born, is a place of special significance in the Muslim world. All Muslims aim to make the pilgrimage to Mecca at least once in their lives.

Mecca, where Muhammad was born and had his visions, is the center of the Islamic faith. The Quran says that all Muslims should, if they possibly can, make a pilgrimage there at least once in their lives. Five times a day, they should also say prayers, facing in the direction of Mecca as they do so.

▼ Muhammad preaches his final sermon. The face has been blanked out since Islam normally forbids all figurative art and particularly portraits of their Prophet or of Allah.

# Buddha

## c. 563–c. 483 BC

The founder of the Buddhist religion was born in what is now Nepal, in the foothills of the Himalayas. He was given the name Gautama Siddhartha. His father was a Hindu.

As a young man, the young prince lived in luxury at his father's court. When he was 16 years old, he married a beautiful princess, and they had a son. But at the age of 29, everything changed for Prince Siddhartha. He suddenly became aware of the poverty and sickness of most people's lives. He asked himself why there was so much suffering in the world.

He left his wife and his home, and spent six years wandering through India. One day, as he sat resting, the answer came to him. Suffering, he thought, was

▲ According to Buddhists, everyone who achieves enlightenment becomes a Buddha. So there are statues of Buddhas all over the world. This one is at Kamakura, Japan.

Buddha's teachings quickly spread from India through southeast Asia, where Buddhism is still strong today. Buddhists spend some time each day in meditation—thinking about the meaning of life—just as their founder did. There are over 200 million Buddhists in the world today.

part of life. No one should complain, because one day everyone would reach the state of happiness and peace called Nirvana. This became the central belief of Buddhism.

Gautama Siddhartha took the name Buddha, meaning "the enlightened one." He collected followers round him, and they went out into the world to teach others. A new religion had been born.

◄ The story has it that Gautama Siddhartha achieved his enlightenment or awakening when meditating under a pipul tree. He sat beneath the tree one evening and by dawn he had become "the enlightened one."

# Moses
## c. 13th century BC

Moses is an important figure in both Jewish and Christian history. The Old Testament of the Bible tells the story of his birth in Egypt at a time when the Hebrew people of Israel were held there as slaves. The Pharaoh had ordered that all male Israelite babies should be killed, but the infant Moses was hidden in bulrushes beside the Nile, where he was found and adopted by one of Pharaoh's daughters.

Moses grew up to become the prophet through whom God spoke to the Israelites. On Egypt's Mount Sinai, God revealed the Ten Commandments to Moses. These laid down the basic laws by which the Israelites should live. God told him to lead his people out of Egypt to the Promised Land of Canaan, or Israel.

The Israelites set out, with the Egyptians in pursuit. Their route led across the Red Sea, where they feared that they would be trapped between the water and the Pharaoh's soldiers. Moses told them that God would protect them. A strong wind parted the waters, and the Israelites crossed. The Egyptians followed, but their chariots were bogged down in the sand. In the morning the waters returned, the Egyptians were drowned, and the Israelites were safely on their way. Moses continued to lead the Israelites for the forty years in which they wandered in search of the Promised Land.

Moses himself never reached the Promised Land, although he saw it from the peak of Mount Pisgah to the northeast of the Dead Sea. There, at the age of 120, he died. It is thought that he was buried close by, but his grave has never been found.

◀ When young Moses was hidden among the rushes beside the River Nile, he escaped death and was found by the daughter of the Egyptian Pharaoh.

# Jesus Christ

## c. 6 BC–c. AD 30

Jesus Christ, the central figure of the Christian religion, was born at Bethlehem, near Jerusalem, about 2,000 years ago. The exact year of his birth is not known. His story is told in the New Testament of the Bible.

Jesus was born a Jew and grew up in the town of Nazareth. When he was about 30 years old, he began to travel around preaching and healing the sick.

Jesus claimed to be the Messiah, or redeemer, that the Jewish prophets had foreseen. But the Jewish leaders of the time did not believe him and he was arrested. They handed him over to the Roman occupiers of the Holy Land, who were worried because his followers were calling him "King of the Jews." He was executed by being nailed to a cross.

Before he died, Jesus asked Peter, one of his disciples, to found a church in his name. In the same year, Peter held the first Christian baptism in Jerusalem. The people who were baptized that day became the first members of the Christian church.

▼ Jesus at the last supper, his final meal with his disciples before his crucifixion.

# Martin Luther
## 1483–1546

In 1510 a young German priest of the Roman Catholic Church paid his first visit to the holy city of Rome. Coming from a poor background—his father was a miner—he was shocked at the greed and extravagance that he found there among the Pope and his cardinals. The priest's name was Martin Luther.

Luther was even more outraged when he saw the selling of indulgences by priests. These were pardons for wrongdoing that were sold in order to pay for even greater extravagances in Rome. Luther was teaching at the university at Wittenberg. One day, he nailed to the church door a statement of ninety-five reasons why the sale of indulgences was wrong. Luther asserted that the Pope could not forgive sins—only God could do that.

Luther had hoped to reform the Church and stay within it, but he was forced out in 1521. The supporters who gathered around him were the founders of the new Lutheran Church, independent from Rome. They conducted their services in German, not Latin, and read from Luther's own German translation of the Bible. Luther, no longer a Roman Catholic priest, married a former nun and they had six children.

Martin Luther's split from Rome was the start of the Reformation, in which Christianity was divided between people who continued to obey the rules of the Roman Catholic Church and those who "protested" against it. Christians who belong to churches that follow the teachings of Luther and his successors are still known as Protestants.

▼ Thanks to Luther's teaching, Protestant alternatives to Roman Catholicism spread across northern Europe. This picture of Luther preaching was painted in Denmark in 1561.

# Johann Sebastian Bach

## 1685–1750

Johann Sebastian Bach was one of the world's greatest composers. He wrote many hundreds of instrumental, orchestral, organ and choral works, including over 300 church cantatas.

Born into a family of professional musicians in Eisenach, Germany, Bach was taught music by his father and later, after his father's death, by his elder brother. He became in turn a choirboy, an accompanist and a choirmaster, and in 1708 he was put in charge of the music at the court of the Duke of Weimar. This involved teaching the choir, accompanying the singing and composing new musical works.

Bach married his cousin Maria Barbara and they had seven children, only four of whom survived. In 1720 Maria died, and two years later Bach married an accomplished singer. Together they had thirteen children, although only six survived infancy. Bach wrote an instruction book for

In his later life Bach was troubled by worsening eyesight, although he was still composing at the time of his death. His blindness was said to have been caused by the long hours he spent as a teenager, copying out music manuscripts in poor light.

his children and a piece for his wife.

After taking various posts, Bach was appointed director of music at St Thomas's Church in Leipzig. He stayed in this post for the rest of his life and during this time composed some of his greatest works, including the *St Matthew Passion* and the *B Minor Mass*. His house in Leipzig became a center of musical pilgrimage, and many leading musicians of the day became his pupils.

Today the music world recognizes him as a brilliant composer of all kinds of music, and as a bridge between the music of the earlier Baroque period and that of the Classical period, which began soon after his time. Bach's music is more popular today than ever.

◀ For about one hundred years after his death, Bach was better remembered as an organist than as a composer.

# Wolfgang Amadeus Mozart
## 1756–1791

Wolfgang Amadeus Mozart was one of the most prolific and outstanding of European composers. He was already writing music by the age of 5, and by the time he was 13 years old had composed concertos, sonatas, symphonies and light operas. When he was only 6 years old, he played the piano for Empress Maria Theresa of Austria and was then taken on a concert tour of Europe's main musical cities.

Mozart was born in Salzburg, Austria, and was taught by his father. In 1771 he became concert-master to the Archbishop of Salzburg, where he stayed for six years. He then moved to Vienna and began to write huge quantities of music. Symphony followed symphony, and opera followed opera. Mozart wrote a total of more than forty symphonies, including the *Jupiter* symphony. His most famous operas include *The Marriage of Figaro* and *The Magic Flute*.

Despite his hard work, Mozart was never free from money worries. Although he had been so much admired in his early years and he always filled his life with work, he was unable to make a living from his music. He had to support his wife, Constanze, and their six children by teaching, but failing health dogged the last three years of his life. He was only 35 years old when he died, a disappointed man. He was buried in a pauper's grave.

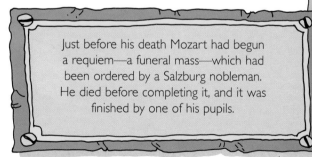

Just before his death Mozart had begun a requiem—a funeral mass—which had been ordered by a Salzburg nobleman. He died before completing it, and it was finished by one of his pupils.

◀ Mozart is recognized as a genius of music, for his great sense of phrasing and melody and his richness of harmony.

# Ludwig van Beethoven
## 1770–1827

As a man, Ludwig van Beethoven was quarrelsome, bad-tempered and difficult to get along with. As a composer, he wrote some of the most beautiful and powerful music of his time.

He was born in Bonn, Germany. He soon showed a talent for music, which was encouraged by his father. When he was 13 years old, he became a professional harpsichordist and organist. In 1795 Beethoven started to write his own music. A successful career seemed assured—and then tragedy struck.

In 1801, Beethoven began to go deaf. The condition was to worsen over the next few years until, by 1817, he was

▼ Beethoven was born in Bonn, Germany, but made his home in Vienna. Here he received lessons from another great composer, Haydn.

Beethoven introduced an idea that was to become very important in orchestral composition. This was the creation of "sound pictures." His *"Pastoral"* Symphony (Symphony No 6), for example, portrays in music the passing of a great storm over the countryside.

completely deaf. Yet very few hints of the despair that he must have felt crept into the music he wrote at this time. It was the period of his first three symphonies and his opera *Fidelio*.

His deafness prevented him from giving piano recitals—his last attempt to do so was a disaster—but he continued to compose symphonies, concertos and sonatas as well as many smaller works. Probably his most famous work, completed in 1824, is his *Ninth Symphony*, whose last movement features a full chorus and orchestra.

# Richard Wagner
## 1813–1883

Richard Wagner spent most of his life trying to make a living from his operas. It was only in the last few years before his death that he achieved recognition.

He was already writing operas by the age of 21, but these early efforts were unsuccessful. The opera houses where they were performed went bankrupt. In 1848 he was forced to flee from Germany because of his involvement in revolutionary politics, and he traveled to France and Switzerland.

Wagner continued to write operas, including those that were later to be recognized as his finest works. But he was unable to get financial backing. Eventually, in 1864, following his return to Germany, he won the support of King Ludwig II of Bavaria, who provided him with the means to have his works performed.

Encouraged by his second wife, Cosima, Wagner combined composing with a plan to build his own opera house at Bayreuth. This opened in 1876 with a production of the *Ring*, Wagner's four-opera masterpiece.

Wagner found many of the stories for his operas in German legends. His hallmark was the way in which he gave each of the main characters a special tune that is repeated each time they appear. He used large orchestras and choruses to create powerful dramatic effects. Wagner's works are now recognized as the peak of opera-going experience.

Wagner died of heart failure on February 13, 1883. Five days later, after his funeral, King Ludwig II of Bavaria rode alone to Bayreuth at dead of night to pay his last respects to the composer whose music he had loved.

◀ A painting of characters from Wagner's *Ring* cycle. The story for this four-part opera is loosely based on an old Teutonic legend.

# Arturo Toscanini

## 1867–1957

Until a little over one hundred years ago, the conductor of an orchestra was not a very important figure in the musical world. People would not go to a concert simply because a particular conductor was going to appear. In the 1880s, this began to change. One of the people responsible was Arturo Toscanini.

Born in Italy, the son of a tailor, he began studying the cello at the age of 9. He was only 19 years old when he started his conducting career in Rio de Janeiro in Brazil. His later career took him back to Italy, and then to Germany, Austria, and the United States.

Toscanini was famous for being strict with his players. He believed that it was not the conductor's or the musicians' job to "interpret," and that they should faithfully follow what the composer had written. The recordings he made are still prized by music-lovers as examples of

conducting at its best, letting the music speak for itself.

Toscanini was one of the first conductors to realize that radio was an ideal means of enlarging the audience for serious music. In 1937 he persuaded the National Broadcasting Corporation of America to create its own Symphony Orchestra to make full use of the broadcasting medium.

Arturo Toscanini's career began with a near disaster. When he made his debut in Rio de Janeiro, the audience set up a chorus of hooting when he appeared. The orchestra persuaded him to ignore it and continue the performance. Once the music began the hooting ceased.

◀ Toscanini was known for his fanatical concern for musical values, and was very strict with orchestras. He was the most tyrannical conductor of his time.

# George Gershwin
## 1898–1937

George Gershwin was one of the few modern composers to write musicals and popular songs as well as works for the concert hall. Gershwin was born in Brooklyn, New York. He was attracted to the music industry as a teenager, and took any jobs connected with it that he could find. At various times he sold sheet music and worked as a rehearsal pianist. In 1912 he wrote his first popular song to words written by his brother Ira. Through the 1920s George and Ira Gershwin wrote a series of popular Broadway musicals, topping the charts with songs such as "I Got Rhythm" and "Embraceable You."

George had already shown his interest in more serious music, and wrote his *Rhapsody in Blue* in 1924 and a piano concerto two years later. These blended a conventional orchestral style with folk music and jazz rhythms, producing a kind of music that became known as "symphonic jazz."

▲ *Rhapsody in Blue*, a work originally written for jazz band and piano, has since become popular with "classical" orchestras the world over. It is a good example of the way Gershwin could cross between the worlds of jazz and classical music.

The invention of "talking pictures"—sound films—in 1928 created new opportunities for the talents of George Gershwin and his brother Ira. Many of their 1920s stage musicals were made into films, and the Gershwins also wrote completely new musicals for the cinema.

◀ In 1937 Gershwin composed the American opera *Porgy and Bess*. The first production was not a success, but it has since become one of his best-loved works.

# Louis Armstrong
## 1898–1971

Louis Armstrong—known to his musical friends as "Satchmo"—was a jazz trumpeter and singer who made his way from poverty to become world famous. Born in New Orleans, the home of jazz, he was brought up by his mother. He learned to play the cornet when he was in a home for children who had committed petty crimes.

When he was released at the age of 16, he started to work with jazz bands in bars and on Mississippi riverboats. At this time he met Joe "King" Oliver, the leading jazzman in New Orleans.

Louis Armstrong is said to have invented "scat singing"—the use of the voice singing nonsense words to serve as an extra instrument in jazz playing. In 1926 he made a record that included scat singing for the first time. Soon, it was being copied by other musicians and became a jazz fashion.

Armstrong moved to Chicago in 1922 to join Oliver's band. It was there he made his first recordings on the trumpet.

For over twenty years, Louis Armstrong was "the voice of jazz" in over fifty films, at countless live performances, on records, and on the series of overseas tours that he began in 1933, working with other leading entertainers. His gravelly voice singing "What a Wonderful World" became his signature tune. His recordings, particularly those of the 1920s and 1930s, are still eagerly sought after by collectors and enthusiasts.

◀ Equally at home on the trumpet or as a vocalist, Louis Armstrong is probably the best-loved jazz musician of all time.

# The Beatles
## formed 1960

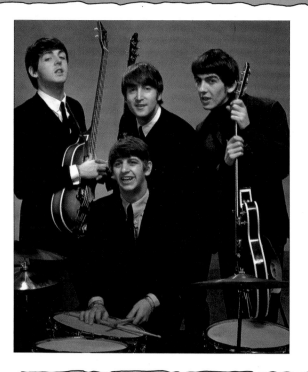

Four young Liverpool men became one of the most successful pop groups of all time. They were John Lennon (1940–80), Paul McCartney (born 1942), George Harrison (born 1943) and Ringo Starr (born 1940). The Beatles sang their own songs, written mainly by Lennon and McCartney. After a struggle to establish themselves, they were "discovered" by Brian Epstein, a local record-shop owner. He became their first manager, and aimed to turn them into national and international stars.

Their first singles, "Love Me Do," "Please Please Me," "She Loves You" and "I Want to Hold Your Hand," were hugely successful. After 1964, when the last two were released in the United States, they became an international success, achieving record sales that had never been known before. They recorded successful albums, appeared in films and made concert appearances worldwide. In 1970 they split up and made their own individual careers.

After the Beatles parted, Paul McCartney and his wife Linda formed a new and successful group, Wings. George Harrison's main interest became film production. There have been constant rumors of the three surviving Beatles recording together again, but so far this has not happened.

▼ The Beatles' success took them all over the world, including India.

# Homer
## c. 700–c.800 BC

Homer was an Ancient Greek poet of whom almost nothing is known except for his poems. Seven different Ancient Greek cities claimed to have been his birthplace. On the Greek island of Chios there is a stone called the "Stone of Homer," where he is said to have sat and recited his poems, but there is no real evidence for this. Homer is said to have been blind, but no one knows whether this was so. Even the exact time at which he lived is uncertain, but most scholars say that it was at some point in the eighth century BC.

This man of mystery produced two long epic (story-telling) poems, *The Iliad* and *The Odyssey*, that are still studied today. Each poem is in twenty-four parts or episodes.

Homer's *Iliad* tells the story of the siege and fall of the ancient city of Troy in about 1200 BC. *The Odyssey* is about the adventures of its hero, Odysseus (or Ulysses), on his long journey back from the Trojan Wars. Among other things, he has to battle with the Cyclops, a one-eyed monster, and fight for his life when his boat is caught in a whirlpool.

▲ The journey of Odysseus took him past the Sirens, sea nymphs whose beautiful singing lured sailors to their destruction.

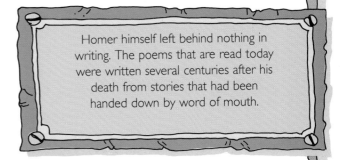

Homer himself left behind nothing in writing. The poems that are read today were written several centuries after his death from stories that had been handed down by word of mouth.

▼ This frieze shows the Greek soldiers finally defeating the Trojans at the climax of Homer's epic poem *The Iliad*.

# Virgil

## 70–19 BC

Virgil was a poet of Ancient Rome whose best-known work is a long epic poem, *The Aeneid*, describing how Rome was founded.

Virgil was born on his father's farm at Andes, near Mantua in northern Italy. All his life, he kept happy memories of his boyhood on the farm, and it provided the theme for many of his early poems.

In 41 BC, when he was 29 years old, he went to Rome, and soon joined a group of poets who were employed by the Emperor Augustus to produce poems for state occasions. Virgil missed his farming home, and he wrote ten poems, *The Eclogues*, that looked back lovingly to country life. Later, he wrote a series of poems called *The Georgics* that dealt with farming techniques. By this time, he had become Rome's best-loved poet.

When Emperor Augustus had the idea of a great epic poem telling the story of the founding of Rome, he chose Virgil to write it. The hero of *The Aeneid* is Aeneas, who, according to legend, traveled from Troy to Italy and created the state of Rome out of the warring tribes that then inhabited the region.

▲ An illustrated version of Virgil's poem *The Georgics* or *Art of Husbandry*, which was written in four books and dealt with tending the land, growing vines and olives, and keeping horses, cattle and bees.

▼ Virgil was the greatest Latin poet in history. His talents were recognized immediately, and his poems became established classics even in his own lifetime.

The twelve books of *The Aeneid* took Virgil eleven years to write. He had almost finished it when he went on a journey to Greece. In Athens, he fell ill and had to return home. He died shortly afterwards.

# Dante Alighieri
## 1265–1321

When Dante Alighieri was 9 years old, he saw a girl called Beatrice Portinari with whom he immediately fell in love. Nothing happened between them. Beatrice grew up, married someone else and died when she was about 25 years old without ever knowing of Dante's feelings for her. But Dante never forgot her, and his love inspired perhaps the greatest work in Italian literature, *The Divine Comedy*.

Dante was born in Florence, the son of a lawyer. Florence was deeply divided in those days between groups of rival families. Dante, having backed the losing side, was forced to leave the city. He spent the rest of his life in exile.

Dante began to write *The Divine Comedy* about five years after he left Florence. This long poem of over 14,000 lines tells the story of Dante's imaginary journey through Hell and Purgatory, with the Roman poet Virgil (see opposite) as his guide, and then to Heaven, where he is guided by Beatrice. On the way, he meets various famous people from history and from his own life. After Beatrice has shown him the wonders of Heaven, Dante comes to understand the meaning of life and death.

▲ Dante stands holding a copy of his poem *The Divine Comedy*. It is thought that he was responsible for greatly improving the Italian language, which was very basic and unformed before this time.

Despite his lifelong love for Beatrice, Dante married another woman, Gemma Donati. They had seven children—six sons and a daughter. The daughter was called Beatrice and became a nun. Dante was buried at Ravenna in northern Italy, where he lived for the last three years of his life.

▶ Beatrice guides Dante on a journey through Paradise in his most celebrated work, *The Divine Comedy*.

# William Shakespeare
## 1564–1616

William Shakespeare's plays are known and enjoyed all over the world. He was certainly the greatest playwright in English, and probably the greatest in any language.

Shakespeare was born in Stratford-upon-Avon, in the Midlands of England. When he was 18 years old he married Anne Hathaway and they had three children. The next ten years of his life are a mystery, but by 1592 he was in London and had started a career as an actor and playwright.

In 1599 he became a theater owner, first of the Globe and later of the Blackfriars Theater, and wrote a succession of plays for his own company of actors. Then, as now, theater audiences were always looking for something new to entertain them. In just over twenty years, Shakespeare wrote thirty-seven plays, including comedies, tragedies and historical dramas, as well as many famous poems.

Shakespeare's plays continue to be popular because of their magnificent, poetic language, and because many of them deal with human problems that are still part of people's experience today. He made sure, too, that even his serious plays provided good entertainment for the whole audience.

▲ Shakespeare is also known as "the Bard," meaning a poet of national importance.

It is thanks to two of his actors, John Hemminge and Henry Condell, that we are still able to enjoy Shakespeare's plays today. In 1623, seven years after his death, they collected and published the texts in what is called the *First Folio* edition. Without their intervention many or all of the plays would have been lost.

# Molière

## 1622–1673

Molière was the name adopted by a French playwright and actor, Jean-Baptiste Poquelin, when he began his career in the theater. He was the son of a wealthy Parisian merchant, and his father had hoped that Molière would join him in the family business. But Molière was already stage-struck, and when he was 21 years old he became a partner in a theater in Paris. By 1658 his company of actors had become favorite entertainers at the court of King Louis XIV of France. Molière wrote, directed and acted in a series of comedies at the royal palace.

Molière's great gift was to use comedy to point out the failings of human nature. He wrote about miserliness, pretension, people who cannot get on with anyone and people who are always suffering from imaginary illnesses. Everyone in the audience knew someone like the people his actors were portraying on stage and so could relate to the play. This was the secret of Molière's success.

The last six years of Molière's life were marred by illness. He refused to give in to it, however, and went on acting in his own plays until the eve of his death.

The last play that Molière wrote, *La Malade Imaginaire*, was about a man who imagines that he is seriously ill. When he wrote it, Molière was truly ill. During the play's seventh performance he almost collapsed on stage. He died the same night.

▶ Molière is considered to be the greatest of all French writers, especially for his comic masterpieces.

# Charles Dickens
## 1812–1870

Charles Dickens was one of England's greatest novelists. He wrote powerful stories about the lives of poor people in the nineteenth century. He knew what poverty was. As a boy, Dickens worked for twelve hours a day in a factory, walking over three and a half miles to and from work each day.

When he was 16 years old, he found work as a journalist. It was another eight years before he achieved fame with the publication of his first book, *Sketches by Boz*. In 1837–9 the first and still one of the best-loved of his novels, *Oliver Twist*, was published in installments. Over the next thirty years it was followed by more than a dozen more novels, together with collections of stories and essays. At the same time, Dickens continued to edit magazines.

For the last five years of his life, Charles Dickens was seriously ill. Despite this, he continued to write and travel. When he died in 1870, he left his last novel, *The Mystery of Edwin Drood*, unfinished.

One of the things that made Dickens's novels so popular was that they were about the lives of ordinary people. Most novelists of his day wrote about the lives of the rich, with whom few readers could identify. He also had a wonderful talent for conveying the way people speak, which brought his characters to life. In most of his novels, humor and tragedy are mixed, so that there is something for every reader's taste.

◀ A painting of *Oliver Twist*, from one of Dickens's most famous novels. Here Oliver is asking for some more food.

# Mark Twain
## 1835–1910

Mark Twain's real name was Samuel Langhorne Clemens. He grew up in Hannibal, Missouri, and worked as a printer, a pilot on a Mississippi river-boat, a soldier and a gold-miner before becoming a writer. In 1867 he traveled to Europe and the Middle East, and his first successful book was a collection of humorous sketches based on his travels.

In 1876, Mark Twain published *Tom Sawyer*, the first of the books by which he is best known today. Written for children, it deals with the adventures of Tom Sawyer and his friend, Huckleberry Finn, in a small town beside the Mississippi River, and is based on Mark Twain's own boyhood memories.

Eight years later, *Huckleberry Finn* appeared. It is a serious book with a more complicated plot than that of *Tom Sawyer*. Many people think that *Huckleberry Finn* is Mark Twain's finest work.

Mark Twain published many other books, but none achieved the fame of *Tom Sawyer* and *Huckleberry Finn*. Later in life, when he was short of money, he wrote two more Tom Sawyer books, but they were never as popular as the original.

Mark Twain took his writing name from his days as a Mississippi pilot. For navigation, the riverboats needed a depth of two fathoms (12 feet) of water. Crewmen would call out "mark twain" if the required depth was there.

◀ A painting from *Huckleberry Finn*. The stories in *Tom Sawyer* and *Huckleberry Finn* were drawn from Mark Twain's own boyhood experiences.

# Bertolt Brecht
## 1898–1956

Bertolt Brecht was Germany's greatest modern playwright. His influence on the theater extended far beyond Germany. After making a false start on a medical career, he staged his first play in 1922 when he was 24 years old. His aim as a playwright was not merely to entertain his audiences but to force them to think about war, politics and freedom.

In 1928 he had his first real success with *The Threepenny Opera*. At about the same time he became a communist. When Hitler came to power in 1933, Brecht was forced to leave Germany and, after moving from one European country to another, went to California in 1941. He stayed in the United States until 1947.

Brecht wrote two of his most famous plays while he was in the United States, *Mother Courage and her Children*, set in seventeenth-century Germany during the Thirty Years' War, and *The Good Woman of Sechuan*. In 1948 he returned to Germany to set up a new theater, the Berliner Ensemble, in East Berlin with his wife Helene Weigel. This brought him worldwide fame.

The unusual style of Bertolt Brecht's early plays, and the ideas they contained, mystified and sometimes angered his audiences. There were riots at the first nights of his first three plays, but one of them, *Drums in the Night*, won a major prize in 1922.

▼ A scene from a production of Brecht's *The Threepenny Opera*, a modern version of the eighteenth-century English *Beggar's Opera*, with new music by Kurt Weil.

# Michelangelo
## 1475–1564

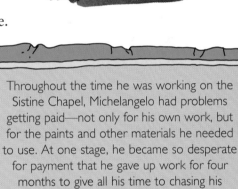

The ceiling of the Sistine Chapel in Rome is decorated by one of the world's most famous paintings. It shows hundreds of human figures and tells the story of the creation of the world according to the Bible. The ceiling was the work of the painter and sculptor Michelangelo Buonarroti.

He was born near Florence, in Italy. When he was 13 years old he began to study painting and sculpture in Florence. Within two years he began to be well known. He went to Rome in 1496, and spent the next five years there. After returning to Florence, he completed one of his best-known works, the statue of David.

He was still only a young man of 28 when, in 1503, Pope Julius II sent for him to return to Rome. Michelangelo's task was to design and build the Pope's tomb. He started this, but he quarreled with the Pope, who ordered Michelangelo to decorate the Sistine

Throughout the time he was working on the Sistine Chapel, Michelangelo had problems getting paid—not only for his own work, but for the paints and other materials he needed to use. At one stage, he became so desperate for payment that he gave up work for four months to give all his time to chasing his employer, the Pope, for money.

Chapel instead. Michelangelo grumbled that he was a sculptor first and a painter second, but he started work. All the time he was longing to get back to his work on the tomb. The tomb, as he designed it, was never completed, but the ceiling of the Sistine Chapel was one of his greatest masterpieces.

◀ The ceiling of the Sistine Chapel in Rome took Michelangelo four and a half years to complete. And for most of that time he was working alone.

# Rembrandt
## 1606–1669

Rembrandt van Rijn was one of the greatest painters in the history of art. He was successful and widely praised, but in his later years he had serious money problems and had to sell his house to pay his debts. He died in poverty.

Rembrandt was born in Leiden, in the Netherlands. His parents sent him to Leiden University, but he soon left and started training as a painter.

In over forty years of working life, Rembrandt produced 600 paintings, 300 etchings and 2,000 drawings. From 1632 he lived in Amsterdam and made his living by painting portraits of leading Amsterdam citizens. He also produced nearly one hundred self-portraits. These are of great interest to art scholars because they show how Rembrandt's style changed over the years.

The middle years of Rembrandt's life brought tragedy. In 1634 he married Saskia, the beautiful daughter of an Amsterdam merchant. Three of their four children died as infants. Saskia herself died in 1642. Although he continued to paint, Rembrandt's life was never the same. His style began to go out of fashion, and his work was less in demand. In 1656 he went bankrupt, and had to move to lodgings in the poorer part of Amsterdam.

One of Rembrandt's most famous paintings was of a group of armed men and used to be called *The Night Watch*. In 1946 the picture was cleaned, and found to be a daytime scene, so it was renamed *The Shooting Party*.

▼ Some of Rembrandt's best works are quick studies he made of scenes around him, like this pen and wash study of the courtyard of a farmhouse.

# Christopher Wren
## 1632–1723

In 1666, a great fire raged for four days through London, destroying four-fifths of the medieval walled city. St Paul's Cathedral and over eighty churches were destroyed.

Britain's leading architect at the time was Christopher Wren. The son of a Wiltshire clergyman, he was educated at Oxford University, where he later became professor of astronomy. From 1663 onwards he turned to architecture, making use of his mathematical skills.

When the Great Fire of London was over, Wren put forward a plan for rebuilding the city. This was not accepted, but he was asked to design a new St Paul's Cathedral and rebuild fifty-one city churches that had been destroyed. St Paul's, his most famous building, took thirty-five years to complete.

Many of Wren's London churches can still be seen, but some were wrecked by the bombing in World War II. St Paul's Cathedral came close to being destroyed by fire, and by an unexploded bomb, but was saved.

Wren also designed many other famous London buildings, including the Greenwich Observatory and Chelsea Hospital, as well as colleges in Oxford and Cambridge. He was knighted in 1672, and for fifty years he was in charge of building work at the royal palaces.

▲ Light pours into the dome of St Paul's Cathedral. The ceiling is a false inner structure, which is much shallower than the outer dome.

When Sir Christopher Wren died in 1723 at the age of 90, he was buried in St Paul's Cathedral. On a stone near his tomb is the simple epitaph, in Latin: "If you seek a monument, look around you."

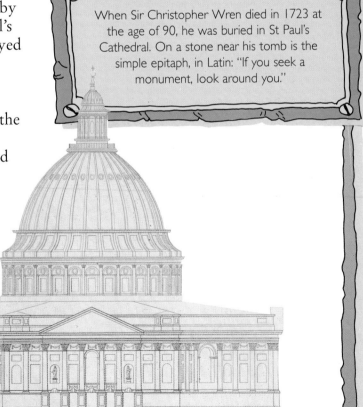

▶ Wren made several designs for St Paul's Cathedral before both he and the authorities were happy. This drawing is his first design.

# Katsushika Hokusai
## 1760–1849

Katsushika Hokusai was the leading Japanese artist of his time, and the first Japanese artist to be widely admired outside his own country. Born in Edo (now Tokyo), he began training as a painter when he was 18 years old. However, he quarreled with his teacher and left the studio where he was studying. From then on, he developed his own techniques and style.

Hokusai chose to live in poverty all his life. Although he also worked as a painter, his great fame came through his colorful prints made from wood engravings in the style the Japanese called *ukiyo-e*. The most famous of these prints are a set of views of Mount Fuji, Japan's sacred cone-shaped volcanic mountain. He completed these when he was in his sixties.

Hokusai delighted in demonstrating his art in public. Once, in front of a large crowd, he painted a portrait on

▲ This bullfinch on a branch of weeping cherry is typical of Hokusai's paintings of natural subjects.

pasted-together sheets of paper laid out in the street, using brooms instead of brushes. Another time, to entertain one of Japan's rulers, he dipped a live chicken's feet in paint and let it create patterns as it ran along a roll of paper.

Hokusai had to be careful in his choice of subjects for his prints. The Japanese government imposed strict censorship on all works of art, and paintings and prints offered for sale had to carry a stamp of government approval.

▶ In this picture Hokusai shows the processions that took place at the Festival of Lanterns. Both the people on the bridge and the boats below carry round paper lanterns.

# Joseph Mallord William Turner
## 1775–1851

JMW Turner was one of England's most famous painters. The son of a London barber, as a boy he sold drawings that were displayed in his father's shop window. Turner was only 15 years old when his first picture was shown at the Royal Academy of Art in London. He became a member of the Royal Academy when he was only 27 years old.

Turner was always attracted by the sea, and many of his most famous oil paintings are of sea scenes. He also traveled widely throughout Europe in search of subjects to paint and draw. His special skill was in the use of strong colors and contrasts to give the impression of light and of the strength of natural forces. A famous example of this is his painting *The Shipwreck*, finished in 1815.

Turner's output of work was huge. When he died, he left 300 oil paintings and more than 19,000 watercolors and drawings to the nation. Many can be seen in galleries.

Turner lived a strange private life. After his father died in 1830, he lived on his own, usually in rooms in inns. He never married and rarely saw his friends.

▲ Most of Turner's pictures were landscapes and seascapes, but he did paint one self-portrait, when he was a young man in his early twenties.

People living near Turner's last lodgings, in London's Chelsea, had no idea that the little old man was a famous painter. When he died at the age of 76—of an illness he did not bother to see a doctor about—he left a large fortune and was buried in St Paul's Cathedral.

◀ Turner could capture the drama of a stormy sea like few other artists. This picture, *Snowstorm: Steamboat off a Harbor's Mouth*, was first exhibited in 1842.

# Vincent van Gogh
## 1853–1890

With their vivid colors and bold brush-strokes, the works of Vincent van Gogh are among the world's best-loved paintings. Yet many of them were produced in the last two and a half years of his life, when he was fighting against insanity.

Vincent van Gogh was born in the Netherlands, the son of a Lutheran Church minister. He spent the first years of his adult life working for a firm of art dealers, and then training to be a preacher. He was 28 years old when he began to study painting. In 1886 he moved to France and spent the rest of his life there. Many of his most famous pictures were painted near Arles in Provence, where he settled in 1888. They include scenes of the orchards, cornfields and cypress groves of the area.

But madness was already overtaking him. After a quarrel with his artist friend Paul Gauguin, during which he threatened Gauguin with a razor, van

▲ A self-portrait by Vincent van Gogh, after he had attempted to cut off his ear.

Gogh cut off part of his own ear. He spent most of the last two years of his life in mental hospitals. He continued to paint up to the day in July 1890 when he shot himself. He died two days later.

Van Gogh's style of painting was not popular during his own lifetime, and he relied for money on his brother Theo, a successful art dealer. Eventually, in the last year of van Gogh's life, a critic praised his work in an important art magazine. But it was too late for van Gogh to enjoy the fame his paintings were finally to achieve.

◀ One of van Gogh's most famous pieces, *Sunflowers*, was painted in 1888 while he was living in Provence, in the south of France.

# Frank Lloyd Wright
## 1869–1959

Frank Lloyd Wright was an American who trained as an engineer and then used his engineering skills to design beautiful buildings. Born in Wisconsin, he was studying at Wisconsin University when a new government building nearby collapsed. This made him realize how closely engineering and architecture were linked. When his studies were finished in 1893 he became an architect in Chicago.

Among his first buildings were long, low "prairie style" houses, but he went on to design larger public buildings such as chapels, hotels, offices, colleges and museums. He was a pioneer of "open planning" —that is, doing away with room divisions so that the spaces inside a building could be used in a variety of ways. Some homes and schools, and many offices, are now built to open-plan designs.

One of Frank Lloyd Wright's most famous houses is "Falling Water," Bear Run, Pennsylvania, designed in 1936. It is built out over a waterfall. The Guggenheim Museum in New York, built in 1959, is another of his designs. The museum's works of art line the walls of a continuous spiral ramp so that visitors can move from one set of exhibits to the next without interruption.

▲ Wright designed buildings that used the latest technology, like these on Rodeo Drive, Beverly Hills, California.

Frank Lloyd Wright's first work was with Louis Henry Sullivan, known as "the father of modern architecture." Sullivan was one of the first architects to design skyscrapers, and quickly realized that these new buildings called for new ideas in design.

◀ Frank Lloyd Wright's "Falling Water" house. Wright produced many controversial designs, and was influenced by the Cubist movement.

# Pablo Picasso
## 1881–1973

Pablo Picasso was one of the most famous artists of the twentieth century. A founder of the Cubist movement, whose followers experimented with different ways of showing reality, his paintings were to be very influential on later artists. Picasso was also a sculptor and worked in ceramics and in collage—pictures made from stuck-on pieces of paper and other materials.

Born in Spain, the son of an artist, Picasso spent most of his life in France. He had his first exhibition at the age of 16. His work moved through different stages as he became more adventurous in his painting. Many art-lovers found his work difficult to understand.

All this changed in 1937 with his huge painting *Guernica*. Its subject was the bombing of the city during the Spanish Civil War, and Picasso's aim was to show the horrors of war and the terror it brought to its victims. *Guernica* was exhibited at the Paris World Exhibition in 1937, when the Spanish Civil War was still raging and Europe was preparing itself for World War II. The art world at last understood that Picasso was a serious artist and not, as many people had thought, a mere showman.

▲ Picasso's *Woman Weeping* shows how the Cubist artists sometimes painted a subject as if seen from several different viewpoints at once.

Pablo Picasso sought any opportunity to experiment in art. Between 1917 and 1924 he designed costumes and sets for the famous Russian Ballet company set up in France by the Russian producer Diaghilev. Later in his life he designed sets for the theater.

▼ *Guernica* showed people the horrors of the civil war in Spain. It also showed that Picasso was an artist with serious intentions.

# Le Corbusier
## 1887–1965

Le Corbusier was the professional name used by a Swiss-born architect whose real name was Charles-Edouard Jeanneret-Gris. The buildings he designed and the books he wrote brought about a revolution in architecture.

Le Corbusier believed that a new style of architecture was needed to take advantage of the new building materials, such as reinforced concrete, that were available in the twentieth century. Architects should look for inspiration, he said, to the design of cars and aircraft, which were built from standard parts for the greatest efficiency. One of his famous sayings was: "A house is a machine for living in." This shocked many people.

In 1923, the year in which he also published his first book, a house near Paris was the first building to be constructed according to Le Corbusier's ideas. He later developed the idea of the

▲ The church of Notre Dame at Ronchamp, France is one of Le Corbusier's most famous buildings.

Modulor, a system of building using standard-sized units that could be assembled in a variety of ways.

Le Corbusier also designed many public buildings, such as the Visual Arts Center at Harvard University in the United States, using revolutionary materials and techniques.

▼ This museum was built in Zurich, Switzerland, in the late 1950s.

Le Corbusier was interested in the design of furniture as well as of buildings. The fitted units found in most kitchens and many bedrooms today are based on his ideas. He also experimented with the use of tubular steel for lounge furniture.

# Charlie Chaplin
## 1889–1977

Charlie Chaplin's "little man"—the character he portrayed in his early films —with bowler hat, ill-fitting suit and his feet-turned-sideways walk, is one of the most famous images of the cinema.

Charlie Chaplin was born in London. He was already an experienced stage performer by the age of 8, and on leaving school he began a career in music-hall. In 1910 he went to the United States, and four years later made the first of many short comedy films, including *The Kid* and *The Gold Rush*. Films had no sound in those days, and comedy had to be made out of gestures, actions and facial expressions.

With the introduction of sound films, Chaplin began to direct as well as act. At the same time, he started to make films with a message, usually a comment on the state of society. His political views were not popular with the United States government, who accused him of having communist sympathies, and in the 1950s he left the country to live in Switzerland. Only towards the end of his life was he welcomed back to America.

▲ Chaplin is seen here in *The Gold Rush*. His films were set in the United States, but the "little man" character was based on people he saw in London.

All his life, Charlie Chaplin kept his sympathy for poor and oppressed people. He knew what poverty was like. When he was a child, his father died and the rest of the Chaplin family were made homeless. They were forced to spend time in a workhouse.

CHARLIE CHAPLIN
IN HIS GREATEST COMEDY
MODERN TIMES

Written, Directed and Produced by
CHARLES CHAPLIN

◀ *Modern Times*, the story of the mishaps of the "little man" working in a modern factory, is an example of Chaplin's films of social comment.

# Jean Renoir
## 1894–1979

Jean Renoir, the son of the famous French Impressionist painter Pierre Auguste Renoir, was one of the great film directors. Born in Paris, he served in the French army during World War I and was awarded the Croix de Guerre, France's highest award for bravery. Renoir started in the film industry as a scriptwriter, but in the 1920s he turned to film direction.

In the 1930s, Renoir directed a series of films that made his international reputation. He was one of the first directors to use natural sounds such as footsteps, train noises and distant, half-heard voices to heighten tension. He had inherited from his artist father an understanding of light and shade, shape and texture, which he used to compose his scenes on the screen.

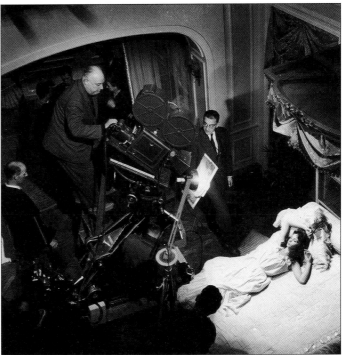

▲ Jean Renoir uses a dramatic camera angle and strong light to create the right effect when shooting one of his scenes.

Renoir wanted his films to do more than just tell a story. His films *La Grande Illusion* (Grand Illusion) and *Le Regle du Jeu* (Rules of the Game), made as Europe was on the verge of another world war, were artistic comments on the state of the world. It was Renoir's style of direction that made people realize that film direction was the work not merely of technicians but of artists.

When Nazi Germany invaded France, Renoir fled to the United States, where he became an American citizen. He continued to make films, including his first dazzling color film *The River*, but it is for his films of the 1930s that he is best remembered.

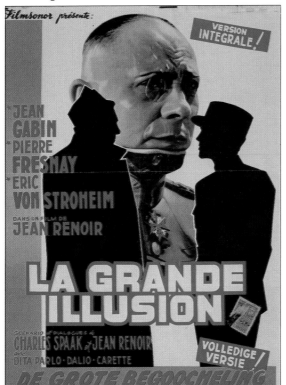

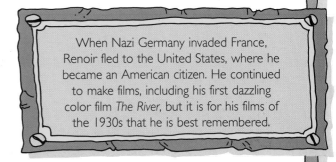

◄ *La Grande Illusion* was made in 1937. It was one of the last films Renoir made before he went to the United States during World War II.

# Sergei Eisenstein
## 1898–1948

In one of the most famous scenes in cinema history, a nanny is at the top of a flight of steps, pushing a pram. There is a closeup of her face. Suddenly, her glasses are smashed. She has been shot. We see her agonized face. Then the picture cuts quickly to the pram which bounces down the steps out of control.

The scene is from Sergei Eisenstein's first and best-known film *Battleship Potemkin*, about a popular uprising in Russia in 1905. Eisenstein, born in Riga in what is now Latvia, made the film in 1925.

Eisenstein developed many new film-making techniques, including montage, in which the film cuts quickly from one picture to another to heighten the dramatic effect. In many of his films, crowds, and

Soviet censorship robbed the world of many Eisenstein films. Between 1929 and his death in 1948 he was allowed to complete only three films, one of which, *Ivan the Terrible*, was not shown in the Soviet Union or outside until many years after his death.

not individual actors, are the heroes and heroines. He was a master at handling crowd scenes, often by cutting quickly from one part of the crowd to another.

Eisenstein made his films in the communist-ruled Soviet Union at a time when there was strict censorship. He could only film stories that were approved by the government. Yet his films are some of the greatest of all time.

THE LONDON FILM FESTIVAL PRESENTS SERGEI EISENSTEIN'S CLASSIC FILM

WITH THE OR[IGINAL] ORCHESTRAL [SCORE] BY EDMUND M[EISEL] PLAYED LIVE B[Y] BRABANT ORCHESTRA CONDUCTED BY ALAN FEARON

1905

BATTLESHIP POTEMKIN

SATURDAY 21 NOVEMBER 1987, 4.00 & 8.00pm
QUEEN ELIZABETH HALL

◀ *Battleship Potemkin* became Eisenstein's most famous film because of its dramatic crowd scenes and its use of the montage technique. The Soviet authorities liked it because it showed the brutality with which the Tsars put down the rebellion.

# Henri Cartier-Bresson
## born 1908

Henri Cartier-Bresson was one of the world's leading photographers, but the camera was his second choice as an artistic medium. Born in Paris, he intended first to be a painter. But when he was about 20 years old he went on a trip to West Africa, taking photographs as he traveled, and this converted him to photography as a means of artistic expression. In 1933 he put on his first exhibition in Paris.

After spending much of the 1930s traveling the world, Cartier-Bresson returned to France. During World War II he was imprisoned by the Nazis. He escaped and spent the rest of the war as a resistance fighter. The return of peace in 1945 made it possible for him to take up his travels again, and he produced a series of books of stunning black-and-white photographs.

The scenes he chose were not posed or planned. He relied on being able to capture on film fleeting moments that tell the story he wanted to convey. One of his collections, published in 1952, was called *The Decisive Moment*, and illustrated his interest in photographing people at important moments in their lives.

Henri Cartier-Bresson was one of a number of photographers working in the 1930s who believed that photographs could do more than merely record events. It was due to their efforts that photography became fully recognized as an art form.

▼ Cartier-Bresson took this photograph in China in 1947. Like many of his subjects, this brush-seller seems unaware of the camera.

# Orson Welles
## 1915–1985

It was evening in the United States. The year was 1938. A radio play went on the air. The play, *The War of the Worlds*, was about the invasion of Earth from outer space. The story and dialogue were so realistic, the play so well-produced, that millions of Americans panicked, thinking it was a true report. It was the first time that most people had heard of Orson Welles, the producer, but it would not be the last.

Welles was born in Kenosha, Wisconsin, and trained as an actor before becoming a radio producer. He then moved into films, and in 1941 he wrote, produced, directed and acted in the film most people regard as his masterpiece, *Citizen Kane*.

*Citizen Kane* is the story of a newspaper owner, whose love of power

LONDON FILMS

One of Orson Welles's finest acting roles was in the 1949 film *The Third Man*, in which he played a racketeer in postwar Vienna. He managed to create an atmosphere of menace without once raising his voice or letting a smile leave his face.

EVERYBODY'S TALKING ABOUT IT!
It's Terrific!
ORSON WELLES
CITIZEN KANE

The Mercury Actors
JOSEPH COTTEN
DOROTHY COMINGORE
EVERETT SLOANE
RAY COLLINS
GEORGE COULOURIS
AGNES MOOREHEAD
PAUL STEWART
RUTH WARRICK
ERSKINE SANFORD
WILLIAM ALLAND

destroys everyone around him. It is told through a series of flashbacks and dreamlike scenes that show just how dreadful the central character, Charles Foster Kane, was to his wife, his friends and his employees. Orson Welles put all his feelings about the American way of life into the film.

◀ Welles directed many other films, and acted in many more, but never again reached the heights of genius that he achieved with *Citizen Kane*.

# Steven Spielberg
## born 1947

Steven Spielberg is the master of fantasy film. Born in Cincinnati, Ohio, he began making amateur films as a child. Having started his career as a television director, in 1971 he moved to the film industry in Hollywood. There, he entered the world of imagination and adventure films, helped by big budgets, astounding special effects and worldwide publicity.

Spielberg's first big film, in 1975, was *Jaws*, the story of a seaside community plagued by a man-eating shark. Two years later he made *Close Encounters of the Third Kind*, in which extraterrestrial beings make contact with the Earth. *E.T.*, released in 1982, dealt with the same theme. A series of adventure films followed, including those featuring the action hero Indiana Jones.

Steven Spielberg's great skill lies in making films that can be enjoyed by both adults and children. He enables families to escape into a world of fantasy that is exciting but not really frightening because it is all too unreal. He has been so successful that he has been able to set up his own production company.

▲ The film *Jaws* catapulted Spielberg's name into the limelight, with its special effects and suspense.

Steven Spielberg's big break, which led to an invitation to Hollywood, came when he made a television film called *Duel* in 1971. It was a simple story, made cheaply using very few actors, about a car-driver who is pursued by a mysterious, apparently driverless, truck. *Duel* showed that Spielberg was a genius at creating tension.

◀ A scene from the film *E.T.* which captured the imaginations of adults and children across the world.

# Euclid

## c. 330–c. 260 BC

Euclid was the Greek mathematician who first wrote down the laws of geometry—the science of lines, surfaces and solids. He founded a mathematical school in Alexandria, where he wrote his thirteen geometry textbooks, called *The Elements*. Every statement made in *The Elements* is accompanied by a method of proving it correct.

*The Elements*, the world's oldest scientific textbook, has had an amazing history. It was translated into Latin, Arabic, English and most other major world languages, and it remained in use in European schools and universities up to the early years of the twentieth century. The first translation into

English was made in 1570 by Sir Henry Billingsley, a London merchant.

Little is known of Euclid's life except for the books he left behind, which include works on astronomy, optics and music. Most of the principles of geometry laid down by Euclid well over 2,000 years ago still hold true today.

There is a story that the Greek Emperor of Egypt, Ptolemy, after struggling to understand *The Elements*, asked Euclid if there was an easier way to understand the subject. Euclid replied, "There is no royal road to geometry." In other words, geometry is hard work whoever you are.

◄ In front of this eighteenth-century engraving of the mathematician Euclid is a book of geometrical diagrams. No doubt many would have been familiar to Euclid, who lived more than 2,000 years before this portrait was engraved.

# Archimedes

## c. 287–212 BC

There are so many stories about Archimedes, the Greek mathematician and scientist, that it is difficult, over 2,000 years later, to separate truth from fiction. He certainly made some important mathematical and scientific discoveries, such as the natural laws governing how levers work. One of his famous sayings was that if he was given a lever long enough and a place to stand he could lift the whole world.

Archimedes was born in Syracuse in Sicily and studied at Alexandria in Egypt before returning home. The story goes that when Syracuse was attacked by Roman forces, he invented a number of weapons to drive them back, including sets of mirrors that focused the sun's rays on the Roman ships' sails, thereby setting them on fire.

Another of his inventions was the "Archimedes screw," a spiral shaft that is still used in some parts of the world to lift water from one level to another. He also studied floating and sinking objects, and discovered the principle, named after him, that describes how water is displaced when a solid object is submerged in it.

He is said to have made this discovery when he noticed how the water level rose when he got into a bath. Legend says that he was so thrilled with the idea, that he ran home through the streets naked, shouting "Eureka!" (I've got it!)

▲ Like many Greek scientists, Archimedes studied in the Egyptian city of Alexandria, which housed the world's greatest library.

Archimedes was killed at the siege of Syracuse in 212 BC, when the city was again attacked by the Romans. It is said that he had ignored the battle because he was intent on solving a mathematical problem that he had drawn in the sand. He was killed by a Roman swordsman.

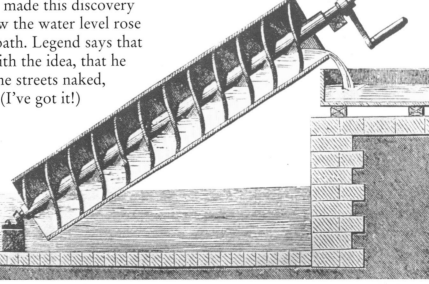

▶ Archimedes screw is a spiral shaft inside a wooden cylinder. When the handle is turned, the water moves up the shaft. The device is still used to raise water for irrigation.

# Leonardo da Vinci
## 1452–1519

Leonardo da Vinci was perhaps the greatest all-round genius the world has ever known. He was a master of all the arts and sciences known in his day, and his imagination enabled him to leap ahead in time to ideas that would have to wait centuries to become realities.

Born in Vinci in northern Italy, he trained as a painter and started his career in Milan. Of his paintings, the *Adoration of the Magi*, the *Last Supper* and the *Mona Lisa* are the best known. He also worked as a sculptor, architect and engineer, and directed entertainments for the court.

In 1500, Leonardo moved to Florence, where he was employed as the Borgia family's architect and engineer. He also found time to continue painting and to study mathematics, anatomy, geology, hydraulics and mechanics. He filled countless notebooks with ideas and

▲ Leonardo da Vinci was a Renaissance genius, he excelled in both art and science.

sketches based on his studies. These show that he foresaw many modern technological developments. His notebooks include, for example, a design for a helicopter.

He went to France in 1516, where he spent his last years as a guest of the French king, Francis I. There, he continued to study and research until almost the day of his death.

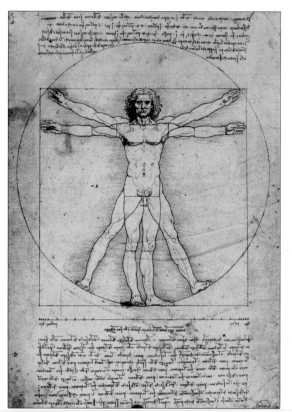

Leonardo's great masterpiece the *Last Supper* began to fade and flake almost as soon as it was completed. It was painted on the wall of a convent. Dampness and chemicals in the plaster, as well as the type of paint Leonardo used, almost destroyed the picture before a method of restoring it was found.

◀ A page of Leonardo da Vinci's notes. He wrote in a strange "mirror writing" and made some of the earliest studies on the workings of the human body.

# Galileo Galilei
## 1564–1642

Until the sixteenth century, scientists still believed most of the theories laid down 1,800 years before by Aristotle (see page 19). But true scientists like to question and check ideas for themselves, and one of these was Galileo Galilei.

He was born in the Italian city of Pisa and entered the university there when he was 17 years old. He intended to study medicine, but soon found that he was more interested in wider scientific questions. While still a student, he experimented with a pendulum and discovered that it could be used to measure time accurately. Galileo's curiosity led him to investigate many different branches of science, but his most famous discoveries were in the field of astronomy.

About a century before, a Polish scientist called Copernicus had suggested that the Earth moves around the Sun, not the other way around as Aristotle had thought. However, Copernicus had no way of proving his theory. In 1632, with the aid of his telescope, Galileo was able to confirm that Copernicus had been right.

▲ Galileo built his own telescope and devoted night after night to studying the sky.

Galileo's discovery that Copernicus was right offended the Catholic Church, which believed in the teachings of Aristotle. Galileo was tried by a Church court in Rome and was forced, under threat of torture, to deny his theories about the Earth's orbit. He spent his last years under house arrest.

◀ Galileo Galilei facing the Church court for confirming Copernicus's view that the Earth revolves around the Sun.

# Isaac Newton
## 1642–1727

In 1665 a great plague swept through England, killing thousands of people. City-dwellers fled to the country. One of those who escaped to the country to avoid the plague was a young Cambridge scientist, Isaac Newton.

Newton went to stay at his mother's farm. During his stay, he began to think about why and how objects move, and why they stop moving. The story goes that this train of thought started when he watched an apple fall from a tree. This led him to discover the law of gravity, the force that pulls objects toward each other. Gravity attracted the apple to the Earth, once it was no longer held on its branch.

From there, Newton went on to work out three "laws of motion."

▲ Newton did much work in astronomy, making observations with this telescope. He made important calculations about planetary orbits.

These explain that an object will stay at rest unless a force makes it move, that how far it moves depends on the strength of the force, and that every movement creates another force which opposes the first. A bicycle moves because its rider applies force to the pedals. The faster the rider pedals, the faster the bicycle goes. But contact between the tires and the road creates another force, called friction, which opposes the rider's efforts.

The investigation of why things move was only one interest. Newton also made important discoveries about light, mathematics and astronomy. For twenty-four years, from 1703 until his death, he was President of the Royal Society, England's highest scientific honor.

DÉCOUVERTE DE LA THÉORIE DE LA GRAVITATION UNIVERSELLE.

◀ Newton himself told the story that the fall of an apple inspired his work on gravity.

# James Watt
## 1736–1819

James Watt was a Scottish engineer who turned the first inefficient steam engine into the power source that drove industry and transport for 150 years.

In 1763 Watt was working as a university technician in Glasgow when a model of the steam engine developed by Thomas Newcomen was brought in for repair. He had never seen such a machine before, and he studied it closely. It used too much coal. It moved in jerks. Most of the energy it produced went to waste. Watt was sure that he could make a better engine.

Within a year, he had perfected his improved version. He then began ten years of struggle to find financial backing to manufacture and sell his engine. At last, he met Matthew Boulton, who had made the older Newcomen engine, and they went into partnership.

Watt died in 1819, too soon to see the full impact of the changes that his invention made to the world. Within the next fifty years, steam engines based on his ideas were providing the power for railways, shipping, the first road vehicles, farm machinery, coalmines, steel mills, and thousands of factories ranging from laundries to printing plants. The nineteenth century was the age of steam power; James Watt was its creator.

▲ James Watt did more than anyone else to develop the steam engine. But his work would have been impossible without the earlier designs of men like Newcomen or the business sense of his partner Matthew Boulton.

Strangely enough, James Watt was not interested in the idea of using the steam engine to power transport. He discouraged one of his engineers from trying to develop a steam-powered road carriage, and dismissed the idea of steam railways as a joke.

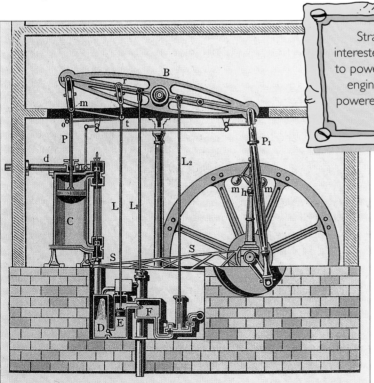

◀ Watt made several changes to make the steam engine more efficient. His twin-action mechanism supplied steam to both sides of the piston, while his governor controlled the engine's speed. His later engines also used a new type of gearing, called a sun-and-planet gear, to make the flywheel turn.

# Michael Faraday
## 1791–1867

If a young bookbinder had not taken time off to look inside the scientific books he was working on, he would never have made his name as a pioneer in the study of electricity.

Michael Faraday became so interested in science that, at the age of 22, he left his bookbinding job for another at London's Royal Institution, then a leading center of scientific research. He worked for a time as assistant to another famous scientist, Humphry Davy.

After doing important work in other branches of science, he specialized in research into electromagnetism—the magnetic force created by the flow of electricity through a coil of wire. In 1831 he discovered electromotive induction, the principle used in electric motors, dynamos and electrical generators.

Michael Faraday was interested only in the laws of science, not in finding everyday uses for them. He left that to others. He stayed at the Royal Institution as the director of its research laboratory for the rest of his life, working with one assistant on a variety of scientific projects.

▲ Michael Faraday is generally thought to be the greatest of all experimental physicists.

While Michael Faraday was working on the theory of induction, an American scientist, Joseph Henry, was carrying out similar research. They worked out the theory at about the same time, but Faraday is credited with it because he published his findings first. Henry became secretary of the United States' leading scientific body, the Smithsonian Institution.

◄ Faraday studied and wrote papers on many topics before he became interested in electro-magnetism, for example: the condensation and vaporization of gases, optical deception and carbon compounds.

# Charles Darwin

## 1809–1882

In 1859 Charles Darwin published a book that shook the world. The result of nearly thirty years of study, it put forward the idea that, over millions of years, all forms of life including human beings had evolved from a few original creatures. Darwin proposed the idea that evolution was governed by the process of natural selection, by which only the strongest creatures tend to survive.

Darwin had begun his research in 1831, when, as a student at Cambridge University, he joined a five-year scientific expedition around the world aboard HMS *Beagle*. He filled shelves of note-books with his observations and sketches, and brought home hundreds of specimens. These formed the basis for his book *The Origin of Species by Means of Natural Selection*.

The twin theories of evolution and natural selection challenged the Bible account of how the world was created. The Christian churches were horrified by these ideas. Darwin was accused of saying that humans were descended from apes— something he had never suggested. Every possible means was used to whip up anger against him.

Charles Darwin lived long enough to see his ideas generally accepted. When he died in 1882, he was granted one of Britain's greatest honors—burial alongside the nation's great men and women in London's Westminster Abbey.

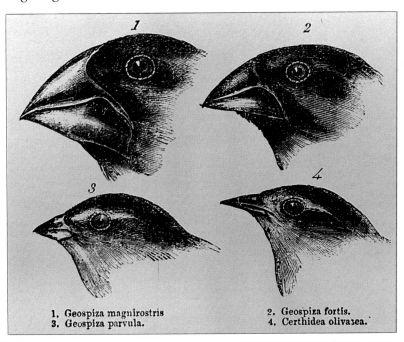

1. Geospiza magnirostris.
2. Geospiza fortis.
3. Geospiza parvula.
4. Certhidea olivasea.

With the support of fellow-scientists, Darwin was able to resist these attacks and develop his ideas further. Few people today question the theory of evolution as Darwin outlined it. He changed the way humankind sees itself.

◀ Charles Darwin made many detailed notes and sketches as he traveled round the world.

# Louis Pasteur
## 1822–1895

In the 1850s, French wine producers were seriously worried. Far too much of their wine was going sour in their cellars before it could be sold. What was going wrong? How could this sourness be prevented? The winemakers turned for help to a professor at Lille University, Louis Pasteur.

Pasteur studied the problem, and found that the wine was being spoiled by tiny organisms that crept in during the winemaking process. He found that these organisms could be killed by heating the wine for a few minutes to a temperature of about 140 degrees Fahrenheit. This heating process is now called pasteurization, and is used to keep other foods such as milk fresh.

This was the start of Pasteur's life's work. Investigating microorganisms or

"germs" more closely, he found that they were a major cause of a wide number of different diseases.

Building on the work of the English scientist Edward Jenner almost a hundred years before, Pasteur developed vaccines to protect humans and animals against a number of deadly diseases, including rabies. Millions of people owe their lives to the knowledge that Pasteur gave to the world about the causes and spread of diseases.

A boy called Joseph Meister was the first rabies victim whose life was saved by using a vaccine developed by Louis Pasteur. Years later, when the Pasteur Institute for Medical Research was opened in Paris, Joseph Meister became one of its first employees.

◀ Pasteur tests one of his vaccines on a dog. He discovered vaccines for rabies and for anthrax, and provided the scientific theory for many more.

# Joseph Lister
## 1827–1912

Up to the mid nineteenth century, hospital operations killed almost as many people as they helped. Patients often died afterwards from infection of their wounds, known as sepsis.

In 1860, Joseph Lister of the Glasgow University Medical School in Scotland decided to investigate the problem. He knew of Pasteur's research into germs, and experimented with soaked dressings with antiseptic solutions of carbolic acid to prevent germs from entering the wounds of his patients.

The results were good, but Lister realized that a better solution would be to kill germs in the operating room before they could reach the patient. He used a pump to spray a mist of diluted carbolic acid into the air during operations.

He also insisted on total cleanliness in the operating room, including the instruments and fittings and the surgeon's hands and clothes. From antisepsis—attacking infection—Lister had moved to asepsis—preventing it.

Before Lister began his work, one out of every three hospital operations resulted in death. After the adoption of his methods the proportion fell to about one in twenty. Methods for achieving asepsis have changed since Lister's day, but his pioneering ideas lie behind the confidence patients have in modern surgery.

Before Joseph Lister's time, surgeons carried out operations wearing their ordinary clothes. They did not wear surgical gloves or masks, and the instruments they used were not sterilized to kill any germs that were on them.

◄ Lister made surgery much safer by introducing antiseptics to the operating room.

# Sigmund Freud
## 1856–1939

Psychoanalysis is a method of investigating and treating mental disturbance, developed by Sigmund Freud, an Austrian doctor. He found that in long, unhurried conversations with patients they would often reveal the childhood memories that lay behind their problems. Once they had brought these memories out into the open, their mental health improved.

Freud had studied hypnosis in Paris. He carefully worked out the best ways of releasing patients' hidden memories. He discovered that dreams, too, had meanings that revealed patients' innermost fears and hopes.

Many doctors ridiculed Freud's views, and even his friends tried to persuade him not to go on publishing his books. But he also attracted support from other doctors and friends, and in 1910 he became one of the founders of the International Psychoanalytical Association. From then on, psychoanalysis became a recognized part of the treatment of certain forms of mental illness. Freud went on revising his ideas and perfecting the techniques of psychoanalysis until the end of his life.

▲ The work of Sigmund Freud covered many areas, from the interpretation of dreams and the psychology of childhood to the study of jokes and their relation to the unconscious mind.

Sigmund Freud and his daughter Anna, who specialized in the psychoanalysis of children, were forced to leave Vienna in 1938 when Austria was occupied by the Nazis. They moved to London where they continued their work. Sigmund Freud died in 1939 and Anna in 1982.

▶ Freud's early work was done in Austria, in Vienna, and here at Riemerlehen, where he wrote The Interpretation of Dreams.

# Albert Einstein

## 1879–1955

German-born Albert Einstein, the greatest scientist of the twentieth century, showed no sign when he was a student that he was going to change the whole basis of science. His teachers were not impressed with him. When he left college, he took a low-grade civil service job in Switzerland and later became a Swiss citizen.

In his own time, without any outside help, Einstein began to study physics. He found that his mind was exploring whole new areas of the subject. In 1905 he published his "special theory of relativity." This states that measurements of time and distance are not fixed, but are changed by movement. It means that, for example, for the crew of a spaceship making a year-long journey into space, time would pass more slowly

From 1913 to 1933 Einstein worked as Director of the Kaiser Wilhelm Institute for Physics in Berlin. He was Jewish, and when the Nazis came to power, he was dismissed and had to leave Germany. He was offered work at Princeton University in the United States. He became an American citizen and lived there for the rest of his life.

than it does on Earth. The crew would even age more slowly!

Einstein went on to put forward other theories about acceleration and gravity, the movement of the planets, the speed of light and the conversion of materials into pure energy. His ideas lay behind such twentieth-century developments as space travel and the splitting of the atom. He was awarded the Nobel Prize for Physics in 1921.

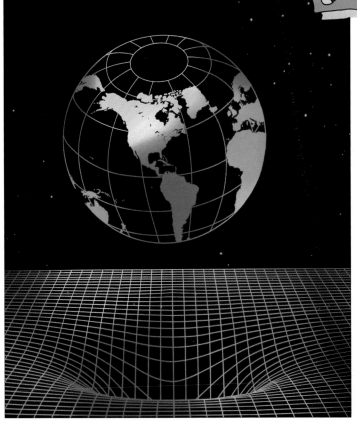

◀ According to Einstein's theories, space is rather like a thin rubber sheet that is warped by the force of gravity. The heavier the object, the larger the dent it makes in space.

# Alexander Fleming
## 1881–1955

If Alexander Fleming had not been a good shot with a rifle, the vital life-saving drug penicillin might never have been discovered. Born in Scotland, Fleming became a surgeon in London. He had been a brilliant student, but it was only because his shooting skills were wanted by the hospital's rifle team that he was offered work in the research laboratory at St Mary's Hospital.

He discovered penicillin almost by chance. In 1928, among a collection of dishes in which he was growing bacteria, Fleming noticed that one had grown a fluffy mold. This had attacked and destroyed the bacteria round it. Fleming published a report of his experiments, calling the bacteria-destroying mold penicillin, but he did not have the knowledge to work out ways of manufacturing it in quantity. For about ten years his discovery went unnoticed.

It was left to two chemists, Howard

Alexander Fleming became a doctor only because his uncle unexpectedly left him some money. He had left school at the age of 13 and was working as a clerk in a shipping company when his uncle died. Alexander's brother, already a doctor, suggested that he should use the money to pay for his studies at medical school.

Florey and Ernst Chain, to develop penicillin to the point where it could be manufactured and used to combat infection in the human body. It was the first antibiotic drug, produced from living organisms. In 1945 they and Fleming were jointly awarded the Nobel Prize for Medicine. By that time, penicillin had become an invaluable tool in the fight against infection.

◀ As well as discovering penicillin, Fleming was also the first to use anti-typhoid vaccines on humans and to discover the antiseptic nature of tears.

# Linus Pauling
## 1901–1994

Linus Pauling was an American scientist who made important discoveries about how atoms combine to form chemical compounds. This process is called chemical bonding. Pauling's work showed how chemical bonding happens, the energies needed to make it happen, and the structure of the compound's molecules.

Pauling was born in Oregon, in the United States. His father died when Pauling was 9 years old, leaving his family with little money. Pauling had to work part-time in order to continue his education, but in 1922 he succeeded in winning a place at the California Institute of Technology. He stayed there, researching and lecturing, for the next forty years.

He began his study of chemical bonding in the 1920s. In 1939 he published a book that gave a full picture of the process. Understanding of chemical bonding helped in the study of abnormal cell formation that leads to illnesses such as leukemia.

In this way, Pauling's work linked chemistry and biology and aided important advances in medicine. In 1954, Pauling's work on chemical bonding won him the Nobel Prize for Chemistry.

Pauling was also famous for work outside his research into chemical bonding. He became convinced that large doses of vitamin C were the key to good health, and wrote several books on the subject. He was also a campaigner against nuclear war.

▶ Pauling won the Nobel Peace Prize in 1962, and became the first person to be awarded two, unshared Nobel Prizes.

# James Watson born 1928
# Francis Crick born 1916

Every living creature, plant and animal, consists of cells made from the cells of the male and female who created it. Each cell contains chromosomes, thin threads of a chemical called deoxyribonucleic acid—DNA for short. Each chromosome contains genes, which carry the information that passes on the characteristics of parents to their children. But exactly how genes work was a scientific mystery until less than fifty years ago.

Two teams of scientists working in Britain found the answer: Maurice Wilkins and Rosalind Franklin in London, and James Watson (an American) and Francis Crick in Cambridge. Wilkins and Franklin studied X-rays of DNA, while Watson and Crick built a model of the DNA molecule. After many false starts, Watson and Crick managed to build a model similar to the X-rays. The model looked like a rope, twisted into a form that the scientists called a "double helix." Inside this structure were millions of atoms which formed the genetic code by which characteristics are passed on.

Watson, Crick and Wilkins were awarded the Nobel Prize for Physiology or Medicine in 1962. Rosalind Franklin died in 1958 before her contribution to the understanding of DNA could be properly recognized.

The discovery of the structure of the DNA molecule opened the way to a whole new branch of science called "genetic engineering." Genetic engineering makes possible the creation of new forms of life by altering the genes in DNA. Scientists can also change the genetic makeup of cells to eliminate or prevent disease.

▼ Watson and Crick work on their model of the DNA molecule at the Cavendish Laboratory, Cambridge, in 1953.

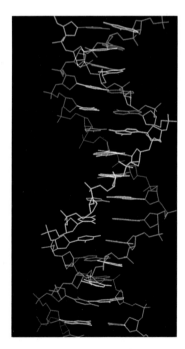

▲ This computer-generated drawing of a section of DNA shows clearly the two spirals (red and blue) which make up the double-helix shape of the molecule. Joined to the helix like the rungs of a ladder are the chemical bases whose sequence makes up a gene.

# Zai Lun
## c. AD 50–118

It is almost impossible for us to think of a world in which there was no paper. Many other materials have been used for writing, such as reeds, animal skins and silk cloth, but the invention of paper allowed the written word to prosper.

Paper was invented about 1,900 years ago in China. Zai (Tsai) Lun was employed at the court of the Emperor of China. He put tree bark, hemp and rags into a vat, and boiled and mashed the mixture into a pulp. Then he lowered a wire or bamboo grid into the mixture. When it was removed, the grid was covered with a thin layer of the pulp. This was squeezed or rolled to remove surplus water and then hung up to dry.

Although, according to Chinese history, Zai Lun was highly praised by the Emperor for his invention, the Emperor's pleasure did not last long. Somehow, it seems, Zai Lun found himself in trouble. Rather than face possible trial and execution, he went home, took a bath, put on his best clothes and poisoned himself.

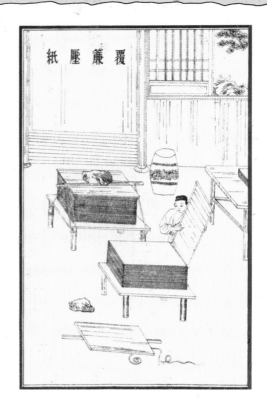

It took about 1,000 years for the art of paper making to reach Europe. Until then, most writing in Europe was done on parchment made from dried and treated skins of sheep, calves or goats. Then paper arrived from the Middle East, and by about 1150 the first European paper mills had started work.

▶ The world's oldest printed book is the *Diamond Sutra*, printed in China in AD 868. The early invention of paper in China meant that they could also produce printed texts—some 600 years before the first printed books appeared in the West.

# Johannes Gutenberg
## 1400–1468

Johannes Gutenberg was a German goldsmith who produced the first European book printed using movable type. Hundreds of years before, the Chinese had used a similar method, but news of this had not reached the West. Western printed books date from Gutenberg's time.

He was born in Mainz. In 1428 he set up in business as a goldsmith. Working in secret, with only a handful of trusted craftsmen, Gutenberg began casting the thousands of separate pieces of type, each carrying a single letter, that he needed to set and print the pages of books. Over twenty years later, in about 1450, his first book was printed. It was a 641-page Bible in Latin, and he sold about 300 copies.

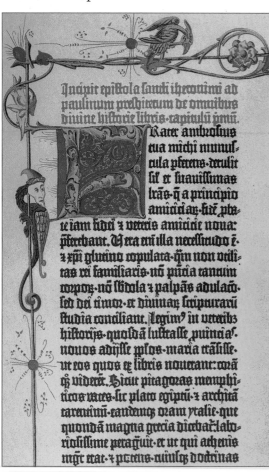

The printing of books in the fifteenth century was not the quick process we know today in which thousand of pages can be printed in a few hours. The first printing presses were hand-operated. Each sheet of paper had to be placed in position, printed and then taken out by hand. It took Gutenberg at least two years to print his first book.

Gutenberg did not get rich from his invention. He was not a good businessman and had fallen heavily into debt. After a court case which Gutenberg lost, Joseph Fust, the man who had lent him money, took over the business. Under Fust's control, the business was a great success, but Gutenberg was forced to seek a pension from the city of Mainz to help him through the last years of his life.

◀ This page comes from Gutenberg's Bible. The text was printed on a press, but the beautiful illustrations were added by hand afterwards—just like an illuminated manuscript of the Middle Ages.

# Samuel Morse
## 1791–1872

A chance meeting on a transatlantic voyage led American-born Samuel Morse to the invention of Morse Code, the first means of communication using electrical signals. Morse, an unsuccessful painter, was returning to America from Europe in 1832 when he got into conversation with a fellow-American, Charles Jackson, about the possibilities of communicating using electricity. From then on, Morse devoted himself to perfecting telegraph communication.

Lesage in Geneva invented the first telegraph, but Morse spent five years developing the project, adding relays and working on his new language, the Morse Code. This consisted of combinations of short and long electrical signals that stood for different letters and numbers. These "dots and dashes" could be sent down the telegraph line as bursts of electricity.

At first, few people were interested in Morse's work. It was not until 1843 that the US Congress agreed to pay for an experimental 80-mile-long telegraph line between Baltimore and Washington. This was Morse's breakthrough. Soon, wires and cables made it possible to communicate instantly across continents and eventually across the world. The telegraph remained a vital means of communication until, at the turn of the century the telephone began to take its place.

S.F.B.Morse.

The first telegraph messages across the Atlantic were sent between Newfoundland and Ireland in 1858. But within three months the cable had broken, and it was not until 1865 that a permanent transatlantic cable was laid.

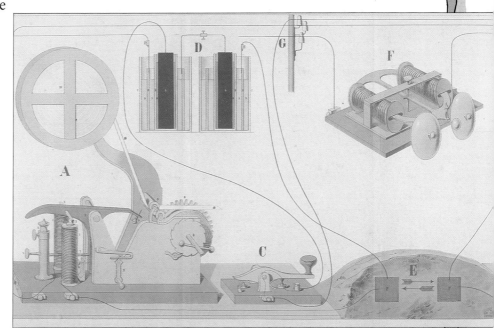

▶ Morse's telegraph allowed his code of dots and dashes to be sent along a wire as short pulses of electricity.

# Nikolaus Otto

## 1832–1891

Nikolaus Otto was a German engineer who invented the four-stroke internal combustion engine from which today's gas engines were developed.

The son of a farmer, Otto left school at the age of 16 and began work as a clerk. He started experimenting with gas engines, using gas made from coal, as a hobby in 1861. His aim was to create an engine that was more convenient and compact than the steam engine, to power factory machines and water pumps. Three years later he turned his hobby into a business in partnership with another engineer.

The first Otto engines were primitive and inefficient, but in 1876 Otto built the first successful four-stroke engine, based on the ideas of a French engineer. In a four-stroke engine, the first stroke draws an explosive mixture of fuel and air into the cylinder, the second stroke compresses it, the third stroke lights it, and the fourth stroke expels waste gases.

▲ Nikolaus Otto, although he had no formal training in engineering, devised the four-stroke cycle that is still used in car engines today.

Thousands of his gas engines were sold to factories all over the world. He left it to other engineers, such as Gottlieb Daimler, to adapt his engine to use gas and to fit it to moving vehicles. Daimler set up his own business, which put the first motorized bicycle on the road in 1886, and a year later produced the first "horseless carriage." But the introduction of the four-stroke Otto engine marked the beginning of a transport revolution.

DAIMLER STAND 54, OLYMPIA
B.S.A. STAND 75, OLYMPIA

Two young engineers who worked at Otto's first factory went on to play an important part in the development of the type of engine used in cars today. Wilhelm Maybach built the first internal combustion engine to use gas, and Gottlieb Daimler built one of the first cars.

# Alfred Nobel

## 1833–1896

War made Alfred Nobel a rich man. He left his fortune to encourage the pursuit of peace and learning.

Born in Sweden, the son of an explosives expert, Nobel moved to Russia with his family when he was 9 years old. After studying chemistry in France and the United States, he went into the family business of making explosives for mining, quarrying and road-building. The explosive then in use, nitroglycerine, was extremely unpredictable and dangerous, and in 1866 Nobel invented a safer form which he called "dynamite."

He went on to develop other new explosives, including smokeless gunpowder and gelignite. These were taken up by the armies of the world and used to manufacture weapons and ammunition. The Nobel factories produced a vast range of explosives for use in peace and war, and Nobel himself amassed a huge fortune.

However, he was an unhappy man who spent his life traveling and seemed unable to settle in one place. He had no children to inherit his wealth, and when he died he left most of his money to endow (or fund) a series of annual prizes to reward outstanding contributions in a variety of fields. The first Nobel Prize was awarded in 1901.

The Nobel Prizes are still awarded each year. They are for physics, chemistry, physiology or medicine, literature, economics and—the best known of all—peace. The winners are chosen by committees whose members are selected by the governments of Sweden and Norway.

▲ This cartridge, packed with dynamite, was made at Nobel's factory in Ayrshire, Scotland. It was cartridges like this, together with other explosive products, that made the money that Nobel left to fund the famous prizes.

# Alexander Graham Bell

## 1847–1922

"Mr Watson, come here. I want to see you." These were the first words ever said over a telephone.

They were spoken on March 10, 1876, by Alexander Graham Bell to his young assistant in their workshop in Boston, Massachusetts. For three years, Bell had been developing his invention, knowing that two other Americans were also working on a similar device. He won the race by just a few days.

Bell was a Scotsman who had emigrated to North America as a young man. He was a qualified teacher of the deaf, and his interest in the telephone arose from his ideas for a hearing aid.

By 1876, however, Bell had become convinced that the telephone could become a means of communication for everyone. He lectured and demonstrated his invention tirelessly, both in the

▲ Alexander Graham Bell makes the call that opens the New York to Chicago telephone line in 1892. Soon telephone lines would cross the United States.

The telephone proved to be a boon to newspaper reporters sending stories from distant places to their offices. The first newspaper story to be telephoned was sent from Salem, Massachusetts, to the offices of the *Boston Globe* fourteen miles away in February 1877.

United States and abroad. Slowly, business and the general public woke up to the benefits of voice communication over long distances, and the telephone industry took off. Bell, meanwhile, tired of it and used his wealth to set up laboratories in which other scientific ideas were developed. But none of these was as successful as the invention that made his name.

◀ Men had to balance high above the city roofs, risking life and limb to erect and repair the overhead lines that made Bell's invention work.

# Thomas Alva Edison

## 1847–1931

Thomas Alva Edison was a giant among inventors. He spent only a few months of his childhood in school and had no scientific training. He learned all he knew from books—and yet he made many of the inventions that we take for granted in today's world.

Edison was born in Milan, Ohio, but his parents were Canadian. His first job when he left school at the age of 12 was selling newspapers and sweets on a train. When he was 16 years old he became a telegraph operator—and this was the start of his life as an inventor. His first projects were improvements to the telegraph system, for which he used his experience of using the equipment.

Edison filed over 1,000 patents for inventions in his lifetime, including the phonograph (an early record player), the carbon microphone and an early movie camera. But his most important work was on the development of electricity as a practical source of power in the home.

In 1879 he invented the electric light bulb, using a cotton filament that glowed when electricity flowed through it. Two years later he installed the first electricity distribution system in the streets of New York. This paved the way for the public electricity supplies that we take for granted today.

Edison's phonograph used cylinders made of tinfoil and, later, wax, on which sounds were recorded and could be played back. The world's first recorded sounds were heard on Edison's machine, although wax discs and the gramophone, invented by Emile Berliner, were later more successful.

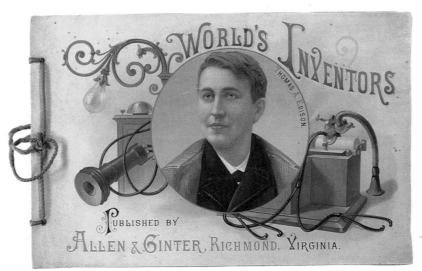

► The phonograph, the microphone and the light bulb were three of the most important of Edison's many inventions.

# Orville Wright 1871–1948
# Wilbur Wright 1867–1912

On December 17, 1903, Orville Wright became the first person to achieve powered flight in a heavier-than-air machine. His flight lasted for only twelve seconds and covered only 138 feet. But it was the start of the age of flying.

Orville and his brother Wilbur lived in Dayton, Ohio. They ran a bicycle business, but for four years they had been trying to build an aircraft. Encouraged by the success of *Flyer I*, as they called their plane, the brothers went on to build an improved version.

The Wrights' flight was a milestone in the history of transport, but few people took any notice. Real interest was not aroused until the Wrights visited Europe in 1908 and demonstrated their aircraft there. In 1909 they set up the world's first aircraft factory in Dayton. Wilbur died of typhoid fever in 1912, and Orville carried on with his work alone.

ORVILLE WRIGHT

WRIGHT BIPLANE

Orville Wright's successful flight was the brothers' second attempt to get *Flyer I* into the air. In the first attempt, three days before, *Flyer I* was piloted by Wilbur. He crashed before take-off. Wilbur was uninjured, and damage to the aircraft was only slight.

▼ The Wright brothers try out one of their aircraft at Kitty Hawk, North Carolina, in 1911. The brothers were always careful to test their machines.

# Guglielmo Marconi
## 1874–1937

The first messages ever sent by radio were flashed across the garden of a country house near Bologna in Italy in 1895. The house was the home of Guglielmo Marconi.

The principles behind radio had already been established by other scientists, but Marconi was first to build a working machine to transmit and receive messages without a wire connection. These were not voice messages—that was to come later. They were telegraphic messages in Morse Code. Because they went through the air, Marconi's system became known as "wireless telegraphy." No one in Italy was interested in his invention, so he took it to England and registered it there.

Armies and navies were quick to see the possibilities of wireless telegraphy, and in 1898 warships of the British Navy succeeded in communicating with each other over a distance of seventy-five miles. The first ship-to-shore wireless messages were sent in 1902, and after that a network of wireless stations was set up at key points to transmit and receive messages from ocean-going ships. Marconi continued to work on improvements to his system, and in 1909 he was awarded the Nobel Prize for Physics.

The life-saving possibilities of wireless were demonstrated for the first time in 1899, when there was a collision between a cargo ship and a lightship in the English Channel. The lightship was equipped with wireless, and was able to send out a call for help.

▼ The military were among the first to see the value of Marconi's invention, and radio played a vital part in communications in the trenches of the western front in World War I.

# Marco Polo

## c. 1254–1324

Seven hundred years ago, people in Europe knew very little about the Far East. A few traders had traveled there and back, but to most Europeans Cathay, as China was called, was a mystery.

The man who opened Europe's eyes to the riches of Cathay was Marco Polo. He was born in Venice, the son of a trader, and went with his father to China when he was about 17 years old. It was to have been a short visit, but Marco Polo became a favorite of Kublai Khan, China's Mongol ruler, and stayed for twenty-four years.

Marco Polo visited India, Burma (now Myanmar) and Sri Lanka as an ambassador for Kublai Khan. He made many journeys inside the vast Chinese Empire. He also took part in the ceremonies at Kublai Khan's magnificent palace. He made careful and detailed notes about everything he saw and everyone he met.

Marco Polo returned to Venice in 1295, bringing with him a fortune in jewels. With the help of a friend, he turned the notes he had made on his travels into a book. This book was widely read, and Europeans were able to learn for the first time of the wonders of China and its advanced civilization.

When Marco Polo returned to Italy he took part in a war between Venice and its rival city Genoa, during which he was taken prisoner by the Genoese. He sent to Venice for his notes, and during his year of imprisonment, wrote his book together with a fellow-prisoner, Rusticiano da Pisa.

▶ Marco Polo returns to Venice with stories of other continents and civilizations.

# Christopher Columbus

## 1451–1506

European sailors in the fifteenth century believed that China was on the western shores of the Atlantic Ocean. Christopher Columbus was one of those who set out to prove it. He was wrong, of course—but his "mistake" led to the European discovery of America.

Columbus was born in Genoa, in Italy, and became a sailor when he was 14 years old. He was convinced that China lay across the Atlantic, and tried to find backing for an expedition to prove this. At last, King Ferdinand and Queen Isabella of Spain agreed to pay for the voyage. In August 1492, Columbus set out with three ships crewed by ninety men.

After eight weeks' sailing without sight of land, Columbus and his men began to get weary. Then, just as they were giving way to despair, they saw timber in the water—a sure sign that they were near land. Soon afterwards, they sighted an island which turned out to be one of the Bahamas.

In later years, Columbus made three more voyages across the Atlantic. He explored much of the Caribbean and landed on the coast of South America.

Columbus never found out the truth about his discoveries. He clung to the belief that the lands he discovered were part of China, and died convinced that he had discovered the sea route to Asia.

▶ Columbus and his crew give praise for the new land, and claim it for Spain.

# Ferdinand Magellan
## 1480–1521

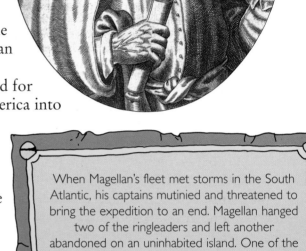

Ferdinand Magellan was the leader of the first expedition to sail all the way around the world, but he died before he reached home. Magellan was Portuguese, but his voyage was paid for by the King of Spain.

He set out in September 1519, in command of five ships and about 250 sailors. They sailed westward across the Atlantic to Brazil, and then headed south along the coast of South America. So far, the voyage had gone smoothly, but now they ran into storms. One of Magellan's ships was wrecked, and another turned tail and headed for home. The rest sailed on around South America into the Pacific Ocean. Another ship had to be abandoned because there were not enough men to crew it. One of the two remaining ships was captured by the Portuguese.

Magellan's ship, the *Victoria*, called at the Philippines to take on fresh food and water, and it was here that their leader was killed in a fight with natives. His second-in-command, Juan Sebastián del Cano, managed to bring the *Victoria* back to Spain with only seventeen survivors.

When Magellan's fleet met storms in the South Atlantic, his captains mutinied and threatened to bring the expedition to an end. Magellan hanged two of the ringleaders and left another abandoned on an uninhabited island. One of the mutineers who was spared was Juan Sebastián del Cano, who survived to bring the *Victoria* home.

◀ An artist's impression of Magellan navigating his ship, the *Victoria*, around the world aided by angels and mystical creatures.

# Roald Amundsen
## 1872–1928

Roald Amundsen, a Norwegian, spent almost all his adult life in exploration. He was the first explorer to navigate the Northwest Passage between the Atlantic and the Pacific oceans to the north of Canada. However, he is most famous for being the first person to reach the South Pole. Yet his journey to Antarctica was almost an accident.

Amundsen was 37 years old when he decided in 1909 to make an attempt on the North Pole, which had not then been reached. But while he was preparing for the journey, news came that the American explorer Robert Peary had arrived at the Pole. Amundsen secretly changed his plans, telling only his brother, and headed for the South Pole instead. He knew that a British expedition led by Robert Falcon Scott had already set out with the same aim, but traveling by a different route, he overtook the British party.

Amundsen's five-man group set out from his base camp in October 1911 on sleds drawn by huskies for what was to be an eight-week journey. On December 14, 1911, Amundsen reached the Pole and planted the Norwegian flag there. He was about four weeks ahead of Scott.

EXTRAIT DE VIANDE DE LA C.ᴵᴱ LIEBIG

LA CONQUÊTE DU PÔLE NORD
5. – Amundsen

Reproduction interdite          Explication au verso

Roald Amundsen gave his life for exploration. In 1928 his friend and fellow-explorer Umberto Nobile disappeared while on a flight over the North Pole in an airship. Amundsen took part in the search, and was killed when his own aircraft crashed in the Arctic Ocean.

▶ Amundsen's base camp in Antarctica, where the party prepare to make their final assault on the South Pole.

# Yuri Gagarin
## 1934–1968

The first person to travel in space was a Russian, Yuri Gagarin. On April 12, 1961, he was launched into space aboard *Vostok I*. He orbited the Earth for almost one hour and a half.

Gagarin could never have dreamed when he was a boy that he would become world-famous. He was born on a farm near Smolensk where his father was a carpenter. When he left school, he took a job in a foundry, but in 1957 he became an officer cadet in the Soviet Air Force. When he heard that the Soviet space program was recruiting skilled pilots to train as cosmonauts, Gagarin applied and was accepted.

Strapped into *Vostok I,* Gagarin reached an orbit round the Earth nearly 180 miles above the Earth's surface. *Vostok I* traveled at a speed of up to 17,500 miles per hour.

After his return to Earth, Gagarin was showered with international honors and given his country's highest award as a Hero of the Soviet Union. But his triumph was short-lived. In 1968 he was killed in an air crash while on a routine training flight.

In the 1960s, the United States and the Soviet Union were locked into bitter rivalry over their space programs. Three weeks after Gagarin's historic space flight, Alan Sheppard became the first American to travel in space.

▶ Yuri Gagarin stayed in orbit for eighty-nine minutes before returning safely to the landing site in Russia.

# Neil Armstrong
## born 1930

"That's one small step for a man, one giant leap for mankind." Those were the words spoken by Neil Armstrong as he stepped from his lunar module. He was the first human being to set foot on the Moon.

Neil Armstrong was born in Wapakoneta, Ohio, and began his career as a fighter pilot in the United States Air Force. In 1962 he was chosen by the National Aeronautics and Space Administration (NASA) to train as an astronaut. Seven years later he was appointed commander of the three-man *Apollo 11* mission to land on the Moon. His companions were "Buzz" Aldrin and Michael Collins.

Collins stayed in the spacecraft command module while Armstrong and Aldrin headed for the Moon in the separate lunar module. On July 20, 1969, they stepped from the lunar module onto the Moon's surface. Through a radio and television link with Earth, millions of people were able to share in the landing and hear his historic words.

Armstrong and his crew returned to Earth four days later, bringing with them samples of moondust and rock. Armstrong later wrote a book, *First on the Moon*, about his experiences on the mission.

▼ As Armstrong and Aldrin walked on the surface of the Moon, they had to get used to the Moon's low gravity, which made them feel lighter than they did on Earth.

The *Apollo 11* Moon landing was followed by five other manned landings before the Apollo program ended in 1972. There have been no manned landings since, partly because of the huge expense involved and partly because the space program has concentrated its resources on other projects such as the space shuttle.

# Puzzle

Solve the clues to fill in the squares across the page. When you have done this correctly, you will find two names or words down the left-hand edge of the puzzle and two down the right-hand edge (clues for these are given at the sides).

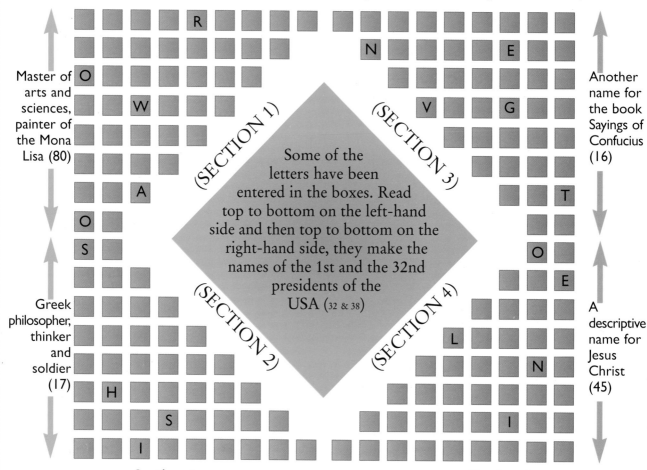

**Master of arts and sciences, painter of the Mona Lisa (80)**

**Greek philosopher, thinker and soldier (17)**

(SECTION 1)

(SECTION 2)

(SECTION 3)

(SECTION 4)

Some of the letters have been entered in the boxes. Read top to bottom on the left-hand side and then top to bottom on the right-hand side, they make the names of the 1st and the 32nd presidents of the USA (32 & 38)

**Another name for the book Sayings of Confucius (16)**

**A descriptive name for Jesus Christ (45)**

## Section 1
1 Nickname of Simón Bolívar, South American freedom fighter (page 34)
2 Someone who sets out to discover new territory
3 Title of one of the epic poems by Homer (page 55)
4 Discoverer of the law of gravity (page 82)
5 3rd century BC King of Maurya, India; known as the "Prince of Peace" (26)
6 Title of cycle of four operas by Wagner (page 50)
7 Chromosomes, which carry genetic information, are made of this (abbreviation) (page 92)
8 Short for opus or operation

## Section 2
1 Thus
2 Alexander the Great came to the throne when he was 20 years --- (page 25)
3 Means of communicating; the Morse ---- uses dots and dashes (page 95)
4 First name of Swedish businessman who saved Hungarian Jews in World War II (page 10)
5 One of the three astronauts on the *Apollo 11* mission to land on the Moon (page 107)
6 Person who values and deals in ideas
7 Discoverer of the theory of relativity (page 89)
8 Producer and director of fantasy films (page 77)

## Section 3
1 Ruler of Tibet, now exiled in India (page 13)
2 Crowned emperor of France in 1804 (page 33)
3 State in the USA where Martin Luther King led a black boycott of buses (page 11)
4 Ancient Roman poet (page 56)
5 The first European book printed using movable type (page 94)
6 Edison's phonograph cylinder was the forerunner of the wax ---- (page 99)
7 Rembrandt was one of the greatest painters in the history of --- (page 64)
8 Part of the verb "to be"

## Section 4
1 Alternatively
2 Watt and the --- of steam power (page 83)
3 A nickname meaning poet for Shakespeare (page 58)
4 English thinker and author of books on knowledge and government (page 21)
5 First name of Japanese rescuer of Jews in World War II (page 9)
6 Humanitarians fight for this basic human right
7 The girl whom Dante loved and who inspired his works of literature (page 57)
8 Founder of religion followed by Ancient Persians (page 41)

Answers can be found on page 111 at the back of the book.

# Index

# Picture Acknowledgments

a = above, b = below

Associated Press: 9; 14
Bridgeman Art Library:
    18b; 20b; 21a; 24a;
    24b; 27b; 28b; 30b;
    31b; 33b; 38a; 44a; 45a;
    45b; 56a; 57a; 57b; 60a;
    62a; 62b; 63a; 63b;
    65b; 66a; 67a; 67b; 68a;
    68b; 70a (c) ADAGP,
    DACS (1995 (Tate
    Gallery); 70b (c)
    ADAGP, DACS 1995
    (Prado, Madrid); 80b;
    82a; 93b; 103b
E.T. Archive: 17a; 25a;
    29a; 29b; 30a; 34b;
    41b; 43a; 46b; 47b;
    48a; 49a; 81a; 81b; 93a;
    101a; 102a; 105
Hulton-Deutsch
    Collection: 10a; 10b;
    36a; 54b; 62a; 91b
Hutchinson Library: 31a

Image Select: 97b (Ann
    Ronan)
Kobal Collection: 73a;
    74a; 76a; 77b
Magnum Photos: 11a
    (Freed); 11b
    (Adelman); 12a
    (Steele-Perkins); 12b
    (Abbas); 40a (Abbas)
    40b (Marlow); 53b
    (Halsman); 75a
    (Cartier Bresson); 75b
    (Cartier Bresson)
Mansell Collection: 19a;
    26b; 28a; 56b; 78a;
    79b; 94a; 98a
Mary Evans Picture
    Library: 8b; 15a; 15b;
    16a; 16b; 17b; 18a;
    19b; 20a; 21b; 22a;
    22b; 23a; 23b; 25b;
    32a; 33a; 35b; 36b; 37a;
    43b; 44b; 46a; 47a;
    48b; 49b; 50a; 50b;
    51a; 51b; 55a; 55b;

60b; 61b; 64a; 78b;
    79a; 80a; 83a; 83b; 84a;
    85a; 88a (Sigmund
    Freud); 88b (Sigmund
    Freud); 94b; 95a; 95b;
    96b; 97a; 98b; 99b;
    100a; 101b; 103a
Mirror Syndication
    International: 35a;
    38b; 39a; 39b; 106a;
    106b
Robert Harding Picture
    Library: 8a; 13a; 13b;
    26a; 27a (C. Bowman);
    31a; 34a (Explorer
    Fiore); 42a; 42b; 52b
    (FPG International);
    54a (FPG Inter-
    national); 64b; 65a;
    66b (British Museum);
    69a; 69b; 71a (Kim
    Hart); 71b (Paolo
    Koch); 85a; 89a
    (FPG International);
    99a; 100b (FPG
    International); 102b;
    107a; 107b
Ronald Grant Archive:

52a; 53a; 62b; 72a; 72b;
    73b; 74b; 76b; 77a
Science Photo Library:
    82b; 89b; 92a; 96a
Spectrum Colour
    Library: 32b; 37b

The publishers would also
like to thank:
Tretyakov Gallery, Moscow;
Duomo, Florence;
Bibliothèque Nationale,
    Paris;
Biblioteca Nationale, Turin;
Vatican Museums &
    Galleries, Rome;
Library of Congress,
    Washington D.C.;
Galleria dell'Accademia,
    Venice;
Courtauld Institute
    Galleries, London
University of London;
Neue Pinakothek, Munich;
Manchester City Art
    Galleries;
Victoria & Albert Museum,
    London.